William Cosmo Monkhouse

The Précis Book

Or, Lessons in Accuracy of Statement and Preciseness of Expression

William Cosmo Monkhouse

The Précis Book
Or, Lessons in Accuracy of Statement and Preciseness of Expression

ISBN/EAN: 9783337186715

Printed in Europe, USA, Canada, Australia, Japan

Cover: Foto ©ninafisch / pixelio.de

More available books at **www.hansebooks.com**

The Civil Service Series.

THE PRÉCIS BOOK

OR

LESSONS IN ACCURACY OF STATEMENT

AND

PRECISENESS OF EXPRESSION.

*FOR CIVIL SERVICE STUDENTS, SELF-EDUCATION,
AND USE IN SCHOOLS*

BY

W. COSMO MONKHOUSE

(BOARD OF TRADE).

FIFTH EDITION.

LONDON:
CROSBY LOCKWOOD AND SON,
7 STATIONERS'-HALL COURT, LUDGATE HILL.
1896.

PREFACE.

The First and Third Parts of this book are the first attempts which, as far as the Author is aware, have been made to extend the principles and uses of Précis-writing beyond 'the Office.'

The primary intention of this book is to provide thoroughly clear, trustworthy, and exhaustive instructions in writing Précis, for the use of those who are preparing for examinations for the Civil Service, and it is hoped that this intention will be found fulfilled in Part II. But the Author's experience has taught him that many persons of full age to be candidates for such employment are, by want of natural aptitude or defective education, incapable of making a short and accurate abstract of even a simple correspondence, though they may be fairly 'educated' in the ordinary sense of the word. It was and is, the Author fears, still a defect in the general system of education in England that boys are not taught to thoroughly understand what they read, or to express what they understand. There are still many boys able to construe any passage in the first book of the Æneid, and yet unable to write in short, simple English a narrative of the events it contains; many more who have 'done' a certain number of lines of Cicero every week for months, if not years, who are incapable of producing accurately one of his arguments in their own language. In many cases the cause of deficiency is not so much want of knowledge as want of power to use it, not so much that the boys do not think as that they have never been taught to express their thoughts.

For those old enough to be candidates it was evidently

useless to endeavour to supply this defect, but it occurred to the Author that it would be a valuable addition to this book if some simple exercises could be devised by which the minds of boys and girls could be trained to habits of order and accuracy in stating the facts of what they know or read, mainly with the view that those who have no natural aptitude for précis-writing may be better able to meet its difficulties when called upon to do so. Hence the origin of Part I., which is designed, as the phrase has it, ' for the use of schools.'

It also occurred to the Author that it might be still more valuable to add some exercises which should extend the use of précis to general reading, and be available to all, without distinction of sex or age, who, from one cause or another, have not acquired the habit of ' marking, learning, and inwardly digesting ' what they read.

On page 182 will be found the commencement of a passage from Locke, which, though not in the mind of the Author before he commenced this part of his work, might well have stimulated him to undertake it. ' Those who have read of everything,' he writes, ' are thought to understand everything too; but it is not always so. Reading furnishes the mind only with materials of knowledge; it is thinking makes what we read ours. We are of the ruminating kind, and it is not enough to cram ourselves with a great load of collections; unless we chew them over again, they will not give us strength and nourishment.' Précis-writing, though not identical with 'chewing over again,' not only requires that that process should be gone through, but furnishes the test that it has been gone through, a test quite necessary to those who, not having acquired the habit of thinking, grow soon tired of it, and easily convince themselves that they have extracted the essence when they are still only grazing the outside. Hence the origin of Part III.

CONTENTS.

PART I.

THE ELEMENTS.

CHAPTER   PAGE

I. INTRODUCTORY.

    Meaning of Précis—Example of it—Its brevity dependent upon its object—Its three principal requirements: Accuracy, Clearness, and Brevity—The term not generally applied to such short abstracts as indices or entries in registers—The simplest form an abstract of facts only—Importance of care in paraphrasing and omission—Its object utility—Précis of the chapter 1

II. ACCURACY.

    Accuracy in facts—Numbers, dates, and proper names—Exercises (A) 7

III. CLEARNESS.

    Handwriting—Importance of legibility, &c.—Foreign and technical words—Exercises (B) 12
    Order—Exercises (C) 18

IV. BREVITY.

    Not to be sought at expense of clearness—List of common abbreviations—Brevity in words—Omission and substitution 26

| CHAPTER | PAGE |

IV. BREVITY—*continued.*
    Exercises (D)—Omission 28
          „   Substitution 30
    Reasons for not giving exercises in abridgment of phrase—Easiness of Précis-writing to some—Its value as a branch of education defined . . . 32

PART II.

PRACTICAL PRÉCIS.

I. LETTERS TAKEN SINGLY.
    Three kinds of Précis: (1) the Register, Docket, and Index; (2) General Précis; (3) Special Précis, with illustrations of each—Different forms—The margin, &c. 35
    Exercises (E) 39

II. SERIES OF LETTERS.
    Instructions for writing Précis of series of letters—Separate and continuous Précis—Examples of both . 49
    Exercises (F)
        (1) 56
        (2) 66
        (3) 73
        (4) 81
        (5) 94

III. PRÉCIS OF A MORE ADVANCED CHARACTER.
    Distinction between foregoing and following exercises—The latter require more thought, power of arrangement, and skill in expression—Importance of mastering subject and the use of fewest and best words, with example 119
    Exercises (G) 121

PART III.

PRECIS-WRITING AS AN INTELLECTUAL EXERCISE.

CHAPTER   PAGE

I. INTRODUCTORY.

    Distinction between practical and intellectual Précis —Value of latter as an aid to composition, reflexion, memory, judgment, conversation, &c.   .   .   . 149

II. NARRATIVE.

    Importance of being sure of main facts of events—Value of Précis for confirming memory, utilising knowledge, and training expression—Instructions as to Exercises, with example 152

    Exercises (H). 155

III. THOUGHT.

    Difficulties of understanding books—Bad habits of reading—Précis-writing a test of understanding—Deceptions of style—Bad styles—Involved style—Verbose style—Clear style—Poetry—Importance of correcting first impressions by reason—Committal to memory not such a safeguard as Précis-writing—Limits of Précis, with illustrations—Précis of poetry —One difficulty exemplified 166

    Exercises (I) 172

THE PRÉCIS BOOK.

PART I.

THE ELEMENTS.

CHAPTER I.

INTRODUCTORY.

THE word *précis* has no exact equivalent in the English language. *Abstract* and *digest* come, perhaps, nearest to it, but there is nothing that expresses that combination of catalogue and abstract of correspondence known in Government Offices as a précis except the word itself.

The following is a very simple example of a précis. We will suppose that Sir Walter Ellicot has privately asked the Secretary of the Board of Sealing Wax why he has had no answer to his letter recommending his butler as Extra Messenger to the Department, and the Secretary, who is absent from the office, asks for a précis of the correspondence to be sent to him in the country. His private secretary would possibly send him something like this:—

Sir Walter Ellicot to Board of Sealing Wax. Feb. 4, 1872. "	Recommends John Thompson, his butler, very strongly for the appointment as Extra Messenger, which he hears is about to be made, and encloses three testimonials.

Treasury to Board of Sealing Wax. March 4, 1872.   Do not think that the Board have shown that necessity exists for an Extra Messenger, and decline to sanction the appointment.

This précis would enable the Secretary to reply to Sir Walter Ellicot without referring to the papers themselves.

In the office of this imaginary Board there would probably exist a still shorter précis of the same letters; for in a Government Office there is no letter, however trivial, to which it may not be necessary to make reference at some time or other, and therefore a Register is kept of every letter which is received, with a very short abstract, or précis, of the contents. These letters would probably be entered in the Office Register in some such way as this:—

Number	Date of Receipt	From whom	Date of Letter	Subject
210	Feb. 5	Sir W. Ellicot	Feb. 4	Recommending John Thompson for appointment as Extra Messenger. 3 testimonials.
415	Mar. 5	Treasury	Mar. 4	Declining to sanction appointment of Extra Messenger

It will be seen that the record, or précis, in the Register is even shorter than the précis supposed to be sent to the Secretary, and the reason of this is that the former is required only as a means of reference to the original papers, and not to supply the place of them, as is the case with the latter.

We will now suppose that, in consequence of further representations from the Board of Sealing Wax, the Treasury at length consent to the appointment of the extra messenger, and the head of the Board of Sealing Wax wishes to have an account of all the applicants for the post, and their testimonials, in order to decide upon whom he shall confer the appointment.

It now becomes necessary to make a longer précis than either of the two already given, which shall give the contents of the testimonials; this précis, in the case of John Thompson, will, we will say, be as follows :—

Sir Walter Ellicot. Stating that he has known John Thomp-
Feb. 4, 1872. son from a boy, and that he has always conducted himself with the greatest propriety. J. T. has been in his service as footman, and then as butler, for nine years, and has discharged his duties zealously and honestly. J. T. is clever, intelligent, and exceedingly methodical. Encloses three testimonials from former employers of J. T.

1. *From Lady Barwell.*—Served as page from January 1852 to December 1854. Honest, sober, industrious, and quick.
2. *From Hon. Arthur James.*—Valet from Feb. 1855 to March 1857. Excellent in every respect; very sorry to part with him.
3. *From Mrs. Bonwell Cross.*—Steward on board her yacht from March 1857 to January 1863. Quite invaluable.

We have now got three précis of the same letter from Sir Walter Ellicot, viz. (1) the précis for the register; (2) the précis necessary for answering the first question; (3) the précis necessary for answering the second question; and the three will show us that the first thing to be considered in writing a précis is the purpose for which it is required, and that its brevity must be dependent upon the fulfilment of this purpose.

It may also be gathered from the foregoing illustration that the three principal requirements of précis-writing are the following:—

    1. Accuracy.
    2. Clearness.
    3. Brevity.

1. Accuracy, because everything depends upon its statements. Whether it be meant for reference or to stand by itself as a substitute for the original papers, it is useless if it cannot be trusted.

2. Clearness, because if there be the slightest ambiguity which makes a reference to the original papers necessary in order to solve it, it fails in its purpose.

3. Brevity, because its object is to save time in reading.

The title of 'précis' is, however, not generally applied to such short abstracts as are only meant to indicate the nature of the contents of papers, such as entries in registers and indices. The following remarks apply only to précis of a fuller kind, the object of which is to make unnecessary any reference to the papers themselves.

The simplest and most common form of what is usually termed a précis consists of little more than an abstract of facts, in which accuracy is the beginning and end, needing neither choice of expression nor abridgment of phrases. The meaning of ordinary letters of business is so clear, and the language so practical, that it is generally impossible to miss the former or alter the latter with advantage.

There is, indeed, nothing in which a précis-writer should be more careful than altering language. It is always safer to use the identical words of the writer of the document abstracted. For the object of a précis is not to improve the style of the writer, but to show what he means; nor so much to shorten his expressions, as to express as shortly as possible his intention. If, therefore, there be the slightest ambiguity in his language, it is preferable to quote his words than to choose one or other of the senses which they may convey, even though the writer's phrase be long and clumsy, for it is better to leave a point doubtful than to run the risk of absolute error. For instance, the word 'expectation' may occur in an important phrase in a letter, and it is nearly three times as long as 'hope,' and is often convertible with it, but if it be not absolutely certain that the writer's meaning would be expressed by 'hope,' the longer word should be used in the précis.

Similar care should also be taken even about omission of words that seem to be superfluous. Though brevity is of very great importance, a word too many is a less defect than a word too few. One word of importance omitted is like a dropped stitch, and spoils the whole piece of work. For instance, a man applying for an appointment may state that he is 'a fair French scholar, and can speak and write the language fluently,' and it may occur to the précis-writer that 'a fair French scholar' will be a short and sufficient description of his capacity; but one man may properly be described as a fair French scholar who can neither speak nor write French fluently, and another may be able to speak and write French fluently without being a scholar, and the capacity of the applicant to hold the appointment may be dependent entirely on his power of writing and speaking, and not at all on his scholarship, or *vice versâ*, or on both.

In other kinds of composition elegance of style, ornament of diction, strength of expression, beauty of form, aptness of illustration, wit, humour, fancy, and imagination may be qualities not only useful, but objects of ambition; but in précis-writing these powers are only useful as aids to understand and interpret the compositions of others. Its object is utility; its most important requirement, common sense.

We are writing now, be it understood, of précis-writing pure and simple—that is to say, the art of abstracting as clearly and shortly as possible the meaning of ordinary correspondence. This is its practical or 'business' side, and though a précis of this kind should be neat in diction and be written in as good English as possible, yet, as long as the sense is preserved and clearly stated, it is possible for it to be little injured by an occasional fault in grammar, or even in spelling, and it will certainly be less injured by defects of this kind than by an inaccuracy in a date, an ambiguity in expression, or the omission of an important word.

Hereafter we shall endeavour to teach the application of the art to abstracts of a literature of a more thoughtful kind than ordinary correspondence, to make the exercises less and less mechanical until the student learns to 'read, mark, and inwardly digest' compositions in which all the qualities of the human mind are exercised, and in the interpretation of which power and even grace of style will not be thrown away.

We must, however, begin at the beginning, and the beginning of the art of précis-writing is the establishment of habits of neatness, thoroughness, patience, and accuracy.

To recapitulate, or, as we may say, to make a précis of this chapter—

1. Précis-writing is the art of abstracting as clearly and shortly as possible the meaning of a composition.

2. A précis will vary in expression and length according to the purpose for which it is required.

3. A précis should be (*a*) accurate, (*b*) clear, and (*c*) brief.

4. A précis should not sacrifice accuracy or clearness to brevity.

CHAPTER II.

ACCURACY.

ACCURACY in précis-writing is primarily requisite in three respects—accuracy in facts, accuracy in arrangement, and accuracy in sense. In this chapter we shall deal only with the first.

Particular care should be taken with numbers, dates, and proper names. A mistake in either of these may lead to great confusion. Official letters have generally a reference number, by which the series of correspondence to which they belong is at once identified. If by carelessness '10,010' is written instead of, let us say, '10,100,' a great deal of trouble may be caused. A mistake in a day may obviously be the cause of similar confusion; and with regard to proper names, especially foreign names, the copying should be especially careful. If 'St. John' is written instead of 'St. John's,' one place being in New Brunswick, the other in Newfoundland; if 'Richmond, U.K.,' is written instead of 'Richmond, U.S.;' or if the ship 'Mary' of London is written 'Marie'—and these are only a few out of thousands of similar blunders that may be made—the value of a précis in other respects accurate may be greatly injured, because the error may cause loss of time in rectifying, and the object of a précis is to save time.

This is the reason why the following exercises for accurately writing and transcribing facts are given.

Exercises (A).

1. Write a list of the pupils in your class, with their Christian names and surnames in full, their position in the

class, the dates of their births (day, month, and year), and the year in which they will become of age.

EXAMPLE.

John Henry Smith, 5th in the class, born August 12, 1865, will be of age in 1886.
James Stephens, 6th in the class, &c.

2. Write the names of any twenty-four articles in the room in which you are sitting, the materials of which they are composed, and the purpose for which they are intended.

EXAMPLE.

Pen	Steel	Writing
Map	Paper	Teaching geography
&c.		

3. Make out a list of your school-books, giving the title, the name of the author, the names of the publishers, the place of publication, the number of volumes, and the number of pages in each volume.

EXAMPLE.

English History, by Harris, published by Williams & Co., at London, in 1872. 3 volumes. Vol. 1 contains 220 pages; vol. 2, 230; vol. 3, 229.
Geography, by Jones, &c.

4. Take a chapter of English History, give its number, and state the pages on which it begins and ends, the reign or reigns which it includes, and the names of any persons or places which it mentions, with the line and the page on which each such name occurs.

EXAMPLE.

Chapter 4.
Pages 110 to 115. Henry III. and Henry IV.
Page 110, line 1. Henry III.
 „   „   „   3. London.
 „ 111, &c. &c.

ACCURACY.

5. Take any country in your atlas, and write the names of the principal places on the coast, stating whether on the north, west, east, or south coast, and the parallels of latitude between which they come.

EXAMPLE.

England, West Coast. Between 54° and 55°. Maryport, Workington, Whitehaven. Between 55° and 56°. Liverpool, &c.

6. Make out a table of the way in which your time is divided at school, showing the hours of lessons, meals, play, rising, and going to bed for each day of the week.

EXAMPLE.

Monday	Tuesday	Wednesday	&c.
7.30. Rise 8.0. Prayers 8.30. Breakfast 9.0. Arithmetic &c.			

7. Make a table of the months of the year, the number of weeks in each, and the days over, with totals.

EXAMPLE.

Month	Weeks	Days Over	Total Days
January	4	3	31
—	—	—	—
—	—	—	—
—	—	—	—
Totals			

8. Make a table of the number of words and letters in each line of the following sonnet, with totals :—

How soon hath Time, the subtle thief of youth,
    Stolen on his wing my three-and-twentieth year!
    My hasting days fly on with full career,
    But my late spring no bud or blossom showeth.
Perhaps my semblance might deceive the truth
    That I to manhood am arrived so near;
    And inward ripeness doth much less appear,
    That some more timely-happy spirits endueth.
Yet be it less or more, or soon or slow,
    It shall be still in strictest measure even
    To that same lot, however mean or high,
Toward which Time leads me, and the will of Heaven;
    All is, if I have grace to use it so,
    As ever in my great Taskmaster's eye.

Note.—These papers should be kept for after use.

CHAPTER III.

CLEARNESS.

Clearness of handwriting is of course essential, for a précis is not only meant to be read, but to be read quickly and easily. It is a matter of comparatively little importance whether the hand be what is called 'elegant' or not, but it should be as legible as print.

Clearness of handwriting should therefore be considered in awarding marks to exercises in précis.

The following hints may not be useless to students who have not practised handwriting with especial regard to legibility :—

The writing should be of a good size, so as not to strain the sight or to require to be looked at close. There should be a clear space between each word and the next, and at least a third of an inch between the lines. Each letter should be carefully formed, n's distinguished from u's, and l's from t's; long tails and loops should be avoided. The general character of the writing should be round and short and upright, and all figures and proper names should be written with the utmost distinctness.

The lines should be straight horizontally, and all commence from exactly the right point. Of course accuracy and clearness in this respect can be ensured by ruling lines down and across the page, but this is an aid which should not be necessary to a neat writer, who should be able to write such a précis as that on p. 3 without any assistance from lines.

Exercises in writing scenes from Shakespeare, and poetry in different stanzas, will be found very useful practice for learning to commence writing a line on the proper spot.

Another of the difficulties to the beginner in writing précis will be found in his want of familiarity with the subject of the letters or other documents with which he has to deal, and with words foreign or technical which are contained in them. We therefore give a few exercises in simple copying, for the purpose of training his eye and hand to transcribe unfamiliar words accurately, and to commence lines on the proper spot. The matter of the following pieces will be further utilised subsequently, so that the space they occupy will not be lost, if the student be too clever a penman to need such exercises.

Exercises (B).

1. Copy the précis on p. 3.
2. Copy the sonnet on p. 10.
3. Diaphenia like the daffadowndilly,
   White as the sun, fair as the lily,
Heigh ho, how I do love thee!
   I do love thee as my lambs
   Are beloved of their dams;
How blest were I if thou would'st prove me!

   Diaphenia like the spreading roses,
   That in thy sweets all sweets encloses,
Fair sweet, how I do love thee!
   I do love thee as each flower
   Loves the sun's life-giving power;
For, dead, thy breath to life might move me.

   Diaphenia like to all things blessèd,
   When all thy praises are expressèd,
Dear joy, how I do love thee!
   As the birds do love the spring,
   Or the bees their careful king:
Then, in requite, sweet virgin, love me!

H. Constable.

4. Under the greenwood tree
Who loves to lie with me,
And tune the merry note
Unto the sweet bird's throat—
Come hither, come hither, come hither!
　　Here shall we see
　　No enemy
But winter and rough weather.

Who doth ambition shun,
And loves to live i' the sun,
Seeking the food he eats,
And pleased with what he gets—
Come hither, come hither, come hither!
　　Here shall he see
　　No enemy
But winter and rough weather.—*Shakespeare.*

5. Absence, hear thou my protestation
　　Against thy strength,
　　Distance, and length;
Do what thou canst for alteration!
　　For hearts of truest mettle
　　Absence doth join, and Time doth settle.

Who loves a mistress of such quality,
　　He soon hath found
　　Affection's ground
Beyond time, place, and all mortality.
　　To hearts that cannot vary
　　Absence is Presence, Time doth tarry.

By absence thus good means I gain,
　　That I can catch her,
　　Where none can watch her,
In some close corner of my brain:
　　There I embrace and kiss her;
　　And so I both enjoy and miss her.—*Anon.*

6. Mr. Owen says, judging from the portion of the skeleton preserved, the Toxodon, as far as dental characters have weight, must be referred to the Rodent order. But from that order it deviates in the relative position of its

supernumerary incisors, in the number and direction of the curvature of its molars, and in some other respects. It again deviates, in several parts of its structure which Mr. Owen enumerated, both from the *Rodentia* and the existing *Pachydermata*, and it manifests an affinity to the *Dinotherium* and the *Cetaceous* order. Mr. Owen, however, observed, that the development of the nasal cavity, and the presence of the frontal sinuses, renders it extremely improbable that the habits of the *Toxodon* were so exclusively aquatic as would result from the total absence of hinder extremities; and concludes, therefore, that it was a quadruped, and not a Cetacean; and that it manifested an additional step in the gradation of mammiferous forms leading from the *Rodentia* through the *Pachydermata* to the *Cetacea*; a gradation of which the water-hog of South America (*Hydrochœrus Capybara*) already indicates the commencement amongst existing *Rodentia*, of which order it is interesting to observe this species is the largest, while at the same time it is peculiar to the continent in which the remains of the gigantic *Toxodon* were discovered.—*Darwin.*

7. Of birds, two species of the genus *Pteroptochos* (*megapodius* and *albicollis* of Kittlitz) are perhaps the most conspicuous. The former, called by the Chilenos 'el Turco,' is as large as a fieldfare, to which bird it has some alliance; but its legs are much longer, tail shorter, and beak stronger: its colour is a reddish brown. The turco is not uncommon. It lives on the ground, sheltered among the thickets which are scattered over the dry and sterile hills. With its tail erect, and stilt-like legs, it may be seen every now and then popping from one bush to another, with uncommon celerity. It really requires little imagination to believe the bird is ashamed of itself, and is aware of its most ridiculous figure. On first seeing it, one is tempted to exclaim, 'A vilely stuffed specimen has escaped from some museum, and has come to life again!' It cannot be made to take flight without the greatest trouble, nor does it run, but only hops. The various loud cries which it utters when concealed amongst the bushes, are as strange as its whole

appearance. It is said to build its nest in a deep hole beneath the ground. I dissected several specimens: the gizzard, which was very muscular, contained beetles, vegetable fibres, and pebbles. From this character, from the length of legs, scratching feet, membranous covering to the nostrils, short and arched wings, this bird seems to a certain degree to connect the thrushes with the gallinaceous order.—*Darwin.*

8. Peter Hopkins could erect a scheme either according to the method of Julius Firmicus, or of Aben-Ezra, or of Campanus, Alcabitius, or Porphyrius, 'for so many ways are there of building these houses in the air;' and in that other called the rational way, which in a great degree superseded the rest, and which Johannes Müller, the great Regiomontanus, gave to the world in his Tables of Directions, drawn up at the Archbishop of Strigonia's request. He could talk of the fiery and the earthly Trigons, the aerial and the watery; and of that property of a triangle—(now no longer regarded at Cambridge) whereby Sol and Jupiter, Luna and Venus, Saturn and Mercury, respectively become joint Trigonocrators, leaving Mars to rule over the watery Trigon alone. He knew the Twelve Houses as familiarly as he knew his own; the Horoscope, which is the House of Life, or more awfully to unlearned ears, *Domus Vitæ*; the House of Gain and the House of Fortune; for Gain and Fortune no more keep house together in heaven than either of them do with Wisdom and Virtue and Happiness on earth; the Hypogeum, or House of Patrimony, which is at the lowest part of heaven, the *Imum Cœli*, though it be in many respects a good house to be born in here below; the Houses of Children, of Sickness, of Marriage, and of Death; the House of Religion; the House of Honours, which being the Mesouranema, is also called the Heart of Heaven; the Agathodemon, or House of Friends, and the Cacodemon, or House of Bondage.

All these he knew, and their Consignificators, and their Chronocrators or Alfridarii, who give to these Consignificators a septennial dominion in succession.

Southey.

9. There was a time when meadow, grove, and stream,
   The earth, and every common sight
         To me did seem
      Apparell'd in celestial light,
The glory and the freshness of a dream.
It is not now as it has been of yore;—
       Turn where'er I may,
        By night or day,
The things which I have seen I now can see no more.

       The rainbow comes and goes,
        And lovely is the rose;
        The moon doth with delight
Look round her when the heavens are bare;
      Waters on a starry night
      Are beautiful and fair;
   The sunshine is a glorious birth;
   But yet I know, where'er I go,
That there hath passed away a glory from the earth.

Now, while the birds thus sing a joyous song,
    And while the young lambs bound
      As to the tabor's sound,
To me alone there came a thought of grief:
A timely utterance gave that thought relief,
      And I again am strong.
The cataracts blow their trumpets from the steep—
  No more shall grief of mine the season wrong;
  I hear the echoes through the mountain throng,
The winds come to me from the fields of sleep,
      And all the earth is gay;
        Land and sea
    Give themselves up to jollity,
      And with the heart of May
    Doth every beast keep holiday;—
       Thou child of joy
Shout round me, let me hear thy shouts, thou happy
    Shepherd boy!

Ye blessèd creatures, I have heard the call
  Ye to each other make; I see

CLEARNESS.

The heavens laugh with you in your jubilee;
 My heart is at your festival,
 My head hath its coronal,
The fulness of your bliss, I feel—I feel it all.
  O evil day! if I were sullen
  While Earth herself is adorning
   This sweet May morning;
  And the children are pulling
   On every side
  In a thousand valleys far and wide
  Fresh flowers; while the sun shines warm
And the babe leaps up on his mother's arm :—
  I hear, I hear, with joy I hear!
 —But there's a tree, of many, one,
A single field which I have look'd upon,
Both of them speak of something that is gone:
   The pansy at my feet
   Doth the same tale repeat:
Whither is fled the visionary gleam?
Where is it now, the glory and the dream?

Our birth is but a sleep and a forgetting;
The Soul that rises with us, our life's Star,
  Hath had elsewhere its setting
   And cometh from afar;
  Not in entire forgetfulness
  And not in utter nakedness
But trailing clouds of glory do we come
   From God, who is our home :
Heaven lies about us in our infancy!
Shades of the prison-house begin to close
   Upon the growing boy,
But he beholds the light, and whence it flows,
   He sees it in his joy;
The youth, who daily farther from the east
  Must travel, still is Nature's priest,
   And by the vision splendid
   Is on his way attended;
At length the man perceives it die away,
And fade into the light of common day.
       Wordsworth.

CLEARNESS in arrangement, or ORDER, is the next essential. This, mechanically considered in relation to précis, consists in little more than the arrangement of correspondence in order of date. This is only difficult when the letters and their enclosures have been mixed up together and require to be sorted.

The best exercises in arrangement are with actual letters, bundles of which may be kept for the purpose; but the following exercises will be of much use in the practice of order, especially if the same care be taken as to accuracy and writing as in the former exercises.

Exercises (C).

[*The following exercises, 1, 2, 3, 4, are to be written from the papers in answer to Exercises (A), which should, as directed, have been kept for the purpose.*]

1. Write out tables of the pupils in the class (1) in alphabetical order, (2) arranged according to age.

2. Write the names of any twenty-four articles in the room, their materials, and the purpose for which they are intended, giving alphabetically (1) the articles, (2) the materials, (3) the purpose for which they are intended.

3. Make out a table of your school-books in alphabetical order, with details in separate columns, in the following form:—

Title	Author	Publisher	Place	Date	No. of Vols.

4. Write in parallel columns, without lines, two alphabetical lists, one of the substantives and another of the

verbs and participles, in the sonnet given in Exercises (A), taking care to write them evenly, as under:—

Substantives.	Verbs and Participles.
Care	Given
Columns	Taking
Exercises	Write
Lines	
Lists	
Participles	
Sonnets	
Substantives	
Verbs	

5. Write the three following lists of words in alphabetical order, the words to be written one under the other, in three parallel columns, one for each set of words, a space being left between words beginning with one letter and those beginning with another:—

(*a*) Rocket, appearance, government, sixteen, Aden, command, propose, visit, report, harbour, admit, vacation, gigantic, peninsula, signal, block, Wales, homage, vanquish, moment.

(*b*) Labour, year, five, almost, whose, triumph, straight, possible, explosion, camp, thousand, eight, proportion, mine, measures, various, banquet, municipal, Gambetta, monsieur.

(*c*) American, chequer, show, dull, school, difficulty, acquisition, upset, previous, fail, attract, congregation, topic, discourse, popular, London, form, discover, response, showy.

EXAMPLE.

(*a*)	(*b*)	(*c*)
Alfred	James	Bexley
Ajax	Jerusalem	Bounce
	Johnson	
Commerce		Candle

(a)	(b)	(c)
Conjugal	Lamp	Debtor
	Long	Dunce
Wexford		
Wigtown	Prussian	Master
Wonderful		Mistress
Word	Quince	
Worsted	Quoit	Xanthus
Woven		
	Zeta	Yellowhammer
	Zoroaster	Young

6. Write the following numbers in numerical order:—

111, 202, 101, 1, 7, 57, 6, 25, 1001, 1101, 2021, 2002, 30034, 3, 20, 100001, 15167, 153, 122, 20000, 1111, 1112, 1212, 1221, 1113, 1376, 75, 4765, 5672, 73461, 8, 92, 526721, 2573601, 18, 126.

7. Do the same with the three following lists in three columns (in the same way as the exercise with words), leaving a space between numbers having a different quantity of figures:—

(a) 15, 100001, 1001, 25, 5768, 2, 54, 726, 8341, 92873, 10, 9864321, 9, 24017, 873.

(b) 2400001, 250002, 7643210, 1001, 10, 1, 240, 6759, 43215, 52768, 81219, 5375641, 2340, 87610, 654321.

(c) 570, 7641, 891012, 52, 176, 99, 999, 9999, 7, 77, 77777, 771, 774, 7775, 77701, 7777.

EXAMPLE.

(a)	(b)	(c)
1	4	2
2	5	180
3	6	
10	16	2000
11	17	2010
12	18	
130	120	30000
140	160	30126
150	170	156789
		246820

8. The following is a précis of the answers received to a plain question addressed to a number of persons:—

Name.	Answer.	Name.	Answer.
Brown, T.	Yes	Ormerod, W.	Yes
Johnson, J.	No	Camroux, P.	Yes
Smith	Yes	Brown, S.	Yes
Robinson	Doubtful	Solomon, A.	Yes
Camroux, S.	No	Quince	No
Antrobus	No	Ranneger	No
Stint	No	Brown, W.	—
Plick, J.	Yes	Thesiger	—
Williams	—	Lilly	Doubtful
Richards	Doubtful	Ormerod, J.	—
Cambridge	Yes	Lee, Thos.	Yes
Plick, T.	Doubtful	Lee, Tim.	Yes
Macready	No	Stuart	—
Joiner, S.	No	Cromwell	Doubtful
Joiner, J.	No	Williamson	Doubtful
Joiner, R.	Yes	Strainger	Yes
Camroux, W.	—	Johnson, P.	Yes
Alick	—	Solomon, B.	No
Thomson	—	Hogg	Doubtful
Ferguson	Doubtful	Dent	—
Pressensé	Doubtful		

(a) Write the names with the answers in alphabetical order.

(b) Give separate lists (each in alphabetical order) of those who have answered (1) yes, (2) no, (3) doubtful, and (4) not at all.

(c) Give the number of each in a separate table with a total.

9. Write out the following précis of correspondence in proper order :—

Oct. 10	Mr. John Grant to Board of Sealing Wax.	Calling attention to previous letter.
Dec. 14	Board of Sealing Wax to Mr. John Grant.	Returning testimonials (11).
Dec. 10	Mr. John Grant to Board of Sealing Wax.	Sending another testimonial and stating that he has the offer of another appointment.
Sep. 10	Mr. John Grant to Board of Sealing Wax.	Applying for appointment of Messenger (10 enc.)
Dec. 13	Mr. John Grant to Board of Sealing Wax.	Requesting the return of his testimonials.
Oct. 12	Board of Sealing Wax to Mr. John Grant.	Stating that application will be considered in due course
Sep. 15	Board of Sealing Wax to Mr. John Grant.	Acknowledging receipt of application.
Dec. 12	Board of Sealing Wax to Mr. John Grant.	Acknowledging additional testimonial and stating that the Board have determined to abolish the post of Messenger.

10. The following exercise is made up of three separate series of letters; write out the précis of each series separately in proper order:—

Mr. Bedford Flood to Admiralty. April 16, 1871.	Stating that he would prefer not to commit it to writing, and asking for an appointment with the First Lord.
Admiralty to Mr. Bedford Flood. May 6, 1871.	Acknowledging receipt of Mr. Bedford Flood's letter of the 5th inst.
Messrs. Anchor & Chain to Mr. J. Makepiece. Nov. 6, 1865.	Stating that they have at length obtained payment of the legacy of 100*l*., and forwarding a P.O.O. for 7*s*. 6*d*., balance after deducting their expenses.
Mr. Henry Harford to Mr. Jabez Israel. June 25, 1858.	Stating that he must decline to give 500*l*. for the Rembrandt.
Messrs. Shackle & Curb to Mr. J. Makepiece. Nov. 4, 1864.	Stating that Mrs. Almond left him a legacy of 100*l*., but it is doubtful whether the estate will be sufficient to pay it.
Mr. J. Makepiece to Messrs. Shackle & Curb. Nov. 1, 1864.	Asking for particulars of Mrs. Almond's will.
Admiralty to Mr. Bedford Flood. May 4, 1871.	Stating that the First Lord has appointed Admiral Jamieson to see and confer with him on the 15th inst., at twelve o'clock.
Mr. J. Fairfield to Mr. Henry Harford. June 20, 1858.	Has seen the so-called Rembrandt, and thinks it a bad copy.

Mr. Bedford Flood to Admiralty. April 4, 1871.	Stating that he has discovered a means of making ships impenetrable by shot and shell.
Mr. Jabez Israel to Mr. Henry Harford. June 23, 1858.	Stating that they never give a pedigree till the purchase is completed, and that his name is sufficient to guarantee the genuineness of any picture.
Mr. J. Makepiece to Messrs. Shackle & Curb. Nov. 3, 1864.	Asking whether Mrs. Almond left him a legacy.
Mr. Jabez Israel to Mr. Henry Harford. June 26, 1858.	Asking him to name a price for the picture.
Admiralty to Mr. Bedford Flood. April 15, 1871.	Stating that they will be glad to receive particulars of Mr. Bedford Flood's invention.
Mr. Jabez Israel to Mr. Henry Harford. June 5, 1858.	Stating that he has a choice collection of old masters for sale, and requesting inspection.
Mr. J. Makepiece to Messrs. Shackle & Curb. Nov. 5, 1864.	Stating that he has placed the matter in the hands of Messrs. Anchor & Chain.
Mr. Henry Harford to Mr. Jabez Israel. June 28, 1858.	Stating that he must decline to buy the picture upon any terms.
Messrs. Shackle & Curb to Mr. J. Makepiece. Nov. 2, 1864.	Stating that the will is not yet proved.
Mr. Jabez Israel to Mr. Henry Harford. June 9, 1858.	Stating that the lowest price for the Rembrandt is 500l.

CLEARNESS. 25

Mr. Henry Harford to Mr. Jabez Israel. June 21, 1858.
Asking for the pedigree of the picture said to be by Rembrandt.

Mr. Bedford Flood to Admiralty. May 5, 1871.
Declining to see Admiral Jamieson, and stating that if the First Lord will not see him he will write to the 'Times.'

Mr. Henry Harford to Mr. Jabez Israel. June 8, 1858.
Referring to his visit to Mr. Israel's gallery, and asking the price of a picture by Rembrandt.

Mr. Henry Harford to Mr. J. Fairfield. June 15, 1858.
Requesting him to call at Israel's and to give him his opinion about the Rembrandt.

11. Write an alphabetical list of all the proper names, and foreign, Latin, or unusual words in Exercises (B), 6, 7, and 8.

CHAPTER IV.

BREVITY.

It cannot be too much enforced on the student that brevity should never be sought at the expense of clearness. The prime object of a précis is that it may be read quickly, and not that it may be written quickly. 'Easy writing' is said to be 'hard reading,' and in the same way it may be said that short writing is very often long reading. For instance, to a person who knows the sequence of months as well as their names it is shorter to write '7/9/75' than '7 Sep., 75,' but not much shorter, while the person who reads may have to count the months on his fingers before he arrives at the conclusion that September is the ninth month in the year.

At the same time it may be very important to economise time in writing a précis, and even space if it has to be sent abroad by post, and some abbreviations are so well understood as to be read as easily as the words in full, and in some cases, as in the case of Christian names, it would be simply waste of time to write the full word. The fact that Zedekiah is the Christian name of a gentleman is seldom of sufficient importance to require more than the initial. 'Z. Smith' is in ninety-nine cases out of a hundred as useful as 'Zedekiah Smith.' The following list of some of the best known abbreviations is therefore given:—

Acknow $\begin{Bmatrix} \text{ledge} \\ \text{ledging} \\ \text{ledges} \end{Bmatrix}$ receipt.   Ack. rec. *or* A. r.

letter   lr̃e.

instant   inst.

ultimo	ult.
proximo	prox.
'ed' at the end of a word	ᵈ.
'ing' at the end of a word, as	ᵍ.
regarding	regard^g.
in the matter of	in re.
circumstances	circ̃s.
'ation' at the end of a word like 'administration'	ŏn. administrŏn.
John	Jn.
James	Jas. or Jac.
department	dep^t.
others	ŏrs.
executors	exŏrs.
administrators	admŏrs.
page	p.
pages	pp.
enclosures	enc.
post office order	P.O.O.
Her Majesty	H.M.

The names of Government offices may generally be represented by their initials—as Foreign Office by 'F.O.,' India Office by 'I.O.,' Board of Trade by 'B. of T.,' General Post Office by 'G.P.O.,' and some of the well-known Companies in a similar manner, as the Peninsular and Oriental Steam Ship Company by 'P. and O.'

The above and similar abbreviations may be used in any of the exercises in this book, but it is unnecessary to give special exercises for them.

Much more important than purely mechanical abbreviations is brevity in words. Two ways of gaining this, though not purely mechanical, are so elementary that exercises in them may well conclude the preliminary course; one is the omission of unnecessary words, and the other the employment of short words for long.

Exercises (D).

OMISSION.

Write the following passages, excluding all words that are not necessary to the sense of the passage, but not altering any of them or adding to them :—

1. O, just give me that indiarubber thing, you know—there, what baby puts in her mouth, you know—baby's ring. It's on the table.

2. All men and women, wherever they are to be found on the face of the earth, have exactly the same features—to wit, eyes, nose, mouth, chin, cheeks, and ears.

3. It is a common remark, and one frequently repeated, that the more knowledge that a man possesses the more he perceives his ignorance, and that every addition to his information adds to his sense of his own mental poverty.

4. Whoever sees himself as others see him can never come to a conclusion as to his real appearance, as no two men ever see him alike, and he will therefore be perplexed by continual variations in his countenance.

5. There is nothing on the earth so thoroughly of this world, worldly, as a woman who, casting aside all higher thoughts, devotes her whole life to raising herself in society.

6. To spell 'immediate' with three m's is an obvious error in orthography.

7. An oak table is a table made out of the wood called oak, and an iron pin is a pin made of the metal called iron; so that we see that the same word is some-

times used as a substantive and sometimes as an adjective, though never at one and the same time.

8. There is—there can be—no pleasure so great as that which has been earned by self-denial, and the surrender of one's own gratification for the sake of duty.

9. A Welsh triad says that the three unconcealable traits of a person, by which he shall be known, are the glance of his eye, the pronunciation of his speech, and the mode of his self-motion—in briefer English, his look, his voice, and his gait.

10. The Indians have an invariable custom, which they always observe, of burying with the dead chief his most favourite horse and best-loved dog, together with his bow and arrows, and also so much food as satisfied him for six weeks on earth.

11. In the very beginning of the year—that is, as soon as the sun rose on the morning of the 1st of January—the priests assembled together to offer sacrifice for the people. The Temple was always so built that it faced the east, and as soon as the sun's face appeared above the horizon the great brazen doors of the Temple were thrown open with a clang, so that its polished walls and the magnificent array of gilded vessels upon the altar might catch the first flash of the sun's glorious beams.

12. The worst of insincere persons is this, that you cannot depend upon them, neither upon what they say nor upon what they will do; they are like the chameleon, who is always changing colour, and whom, though you have left him of a bright red, you may find on your return of a dull green—but with this difference, that the changes in colour of the chameleon are involuntary, while the changes of the insincere man are conscious.

SUBSTITUTING SHORT WORDS FOR LONG.

Shorten the following passages by omission, or by substituting short words for long, or one word for two, without altering the order or construction of the sentences:—

1. Every description of article will be discovered in this repository.
2. The miserable slaves were connected with chains.
3. The result exceeded our expectations.
4. He considered that the universe was spherical.
5. He endeavoured to proceed in the opposite direction.
6. Security promptly invigorated a mind enfeebled by idle perturbations.
7. Now, wherefore have I entitled this book 'The Heroes'? Because that was the appellation which the Hellens gave to men who were courageous and skilful, and dare do more than other individuals. At first, I imagine, that was all it meant; but after a time it came to mean something in addition; it came to mean men who assisted their country; men in those ancient times, when the country was half savage, who killed ferocious beasts and evil men, and drained swamps, and established towns, and therefore, after they were defunct, were honoured, because they had left their country better than they found it. And we call a man a hero in English to this day, and call it a 'heroic' thing to suffer pain and sorrow, that we may obtain advantage for our fellow-mortals.—*Altered from Kingsley.*

8 Then a mighty awe descended upon Perseus; and he went out in the morning to the populace, and narrated his vision, and bade them build altars to Zeus, the Father

of Divine and human beings, and to Athené, who gives sapience to heroes, and be no more afraid of the earthquakes and the floods, but sow and build in tranquillity. And they acted in this way for a while, and prospered; but after Perseus had departed they forgot Zeus and Athené, and worshipped once again Atergatis the Queen, and the never-dying fish of the consecrated lake, where Deucalion's deluge was swallowed up, and they burnt their children before the Fire King, till Zeus was irritated against that foolish people, and brought a strange nation out of Egypt who fought against them and despoiled them altogether, and resided in their cities for a great many hundred years.—*Altered from Kingsley.*

9. The Arabs have a singular manner of displaying their courage in engagements, not unlike the devotement to the infernal gods among the ancients. A soldier willing to signalise his attachment to his master binds up his leg to his thigh, and continues to fire away upon the enemy, till either they be routed, or he himself be slain upon the field of battle.

10. But if we would construct a judgment of the internal contents of that portentous head which is thus formidably adumbrated, how could it be done so well as by beholding the Doctor among his books, and there beholding the victuals upon which his terrific intellect is supported? There we should behold the accents, dialects, digammas, and other such small gear as in these days constitute the complete armour of a perfect scholar.—*Southey.*

11. In goodness of heart, and in principles of piety, this exemplary couple was bound to each other by the most perfect unison of character, though in their tempers there was a contrast which had scarce the gradation of a single shade to smooth off its abrupt dissimilitude. Mr. Tyrold, gentle with wisdom, and benign in virtue, saw with

compassion all imperfections but his own. Yet the mildness that urged him to pity blinded him not to approve; his equity was unerring though his judgment was indulgent. His partner had a firmness of mind which nothing could shake: calamity found her resolute; even prosperity was powerless to lull her duties asleep. The exalted character of her husband was the pride of her existence and the source of her happiness. He was not merely her standard of excellence, but of endurance, since her sense of his worth was the criterion for her opinion of all others. This instigated a spirit of comparison, which is almost always uncandid, and which here could rarely escape proving injurious. Such at its very best is the unskilfulness of our fallible nature, that even the noble principle which impels our love of right misleads us but into new deviations, when its ambition presumes to point at perfection. In this instance, however, distinctness of disposition did not stifle reciprocity of affection—that magnetic concentration of all marriage felicity. Mr. Tyrold revered while he softened the rigid virtues of his wife, who adored while she fortified the melting humanity of her husband.—*Miss Burney.*

The last piece cannot be abridged as much as it should be without shortening it in other ways than by the mere omission of words and substitution of long words for short. To do it thoroughly it should be recast, and nearly every sentence remodelled, and abridged by the constant substitution of one word for a good many. It will be a good test of the aptitude of the pupil for précis-writing of the higher kind to try to reproduce the sense of the passage in as few words as possible.

We might here give some examples and exercises of this more thorough style of abridgment, but we forbear to do so. 1. Because the abridgment of 'phrases of a complicated kind is seldom required in ordinary précis-writing, official or business documents being rarely verbose or tautological. 2. It will be more in due intellectual order for the student to learn how to make an abstract of facts and the sense of documents before he turns his attention to the concentration of style. 3. Because, though terse writing is the object of précis-writing, it can only be gained by experience, and it will come of itself to those who have the smallest aptitude before they have finished the exercises in this book.

The art of précis-writing of this higher kind comes, indeed, so easily to those who have a natural aptitude for seizing the sense of what they read and expressing it in a short simple way, and is so difficult of acquirement by others, that at first sight it would seem that to those who have such a natural aptitude instruction is unnecessary, and that to those who have not it is useless.

And so no doubt it would be if men and women could be divided into two such companies, like sheep and goats, or, in other words, if that aptitude which we have called natural was not as much the result of early training as of innate faculty. There is no doubt that some persons learn how to think and express what they mean much more easily than others, but there is also no doubt that a mind must be exceptionally dull if it cannot be taught to do both, and anyone who has these faculties can also apprehend the meaning of what other people write, and reproduce it in another form, if the subject and style be not above their comprehension, and they have a tolerable acquaintance with their language.

The art of précis-writing is not the art of original thought, or even the art of comprehension of others' thoughts, but it is a test of the latter and a valuable aid to the former, for it requires the habit of reflection.—

'reading, marking, and inwardly digesting,' as the collect has it—and also of reproduction.

To illustrate what we mean, let the reader try to write a précis of the three paragraphs we have already written, and if he thoroughly understands them he will have little difficulty in reproducing their sense in some such form as this :—

Précis-writing comes so easily to some, and so hardly to others, that it would seem as if instruction were unnecessary or useless.

So it would be if it were an entirely natural gift, but it is not. Some persons can be taught to think and talk more easily than others, but all persons can be taught to think and talk, and those who can do these things can also read and write précis, if they have been educated.

Précis-writing is a different exercise from that of thinking, or even comprehension, but it shows whether you comprehend and teaches you to think.

PART II.
PRACTICAL PRÉCIS.

CHAPTER I.

LETTERS TAKEN SINGLY.

In the Introduction we have given an instance of one letter of which three abstracts were required, each slightly differing from the other in accordance with the purpose for which it was intended, and though the length, form, and character of a précis may vary almost infinitely according to this purpose, it is safe to say that précis may be divided into three kinds—

1. *The register, docket, or index,* for purposes of reference only, so as to enable a person to discover the letter to which he wishes to refer.

2. *The précis for general purposes,* which is intended to be as useful for most purposes as the correspondence itself, and should therefore be as full but as brief as possible.

3. *The précis for a special purpose,* from which all matter should be excluded irrelevant to that special purpose. This, it is evident, may vary in length from the briefest to the fullest précis, according to what that purpose is.

It may be objected that the first of these three is not a précis at all, but rather of the nature of an index; but insomuch as it is more than what is usually termed an index, containing as it does an abstract, though a very brief one, of the contents of a document, it has a claim to be considered as the most elementary form of a précis, and it will, we think, help the student to a clearer view of the object of précis-writing generally if he so consider it.

The Docket, Register Entry, or Index.

These three names express three different forms of the same description of elementary précis required for three different purposes.

1. *The Docket, or endorsement of a paper.*—When papers are kept folded, an abstract of the contents is written on the back of each letter in some such form as this :—

Feb. 3, 1875.

Mr. Layard

Has represented to Señor
Canovas the sentiments of H.M.
Government on the accession
of King Alfonso.

1 enclosure.
Received Feb. 14, 1874.

2. *The Register Entry.*—This is a copy of the Docket as entered in the Register Book of the Office, in some such form as this :—

Date of Receipt	Correspondent	Date of Letter	Subject
Feb. 14	Mr. Layard	Feb. 3	Has represented to Señor Canovas, &c.

3. *The Index.*—This is only required when a correspondence is published. The letters are then numbered and indexed in this way:—

| 4 | Mr. Layard to Foreign Office | Feb. 3, 1874 | Has represented to Señor Canovas, &c. |

The Special and General Précis.

The forms of these are similar, and the best for both is this:—

Mr. Layard to Foreign Office. Feb. 3, 1874.   Has represented to Señor Canovas the sentiments of H.M. Government on the accession of King Alfonso, and given him a memorandum (copy enclosed) of what he said. Señor Canovas replied that the King and Government would appreciate the interest shown by H.M. Government in the King and his nation, stated that the friendship of England was dear to Spain, and repeated assurances of his intention to maintain religious freedom.

This is a general précis of the following extract:—

Mr. Layard to the Earl of Derby.
(Received February 14.)
MADRID : February 3, 1875.

I called upon Señor Canovas del Castillo yesterday, and communicated to his Excellency the substance of your Lordship's despatch of the 26th ultimo. As your Lordship had left it to me to convey this expression of the sentiments of Her Majesty's Government to that of the King in the manner which might appear to me most suitable, I thought it best to do so to the President of the

Ministry Regent. In order that there should be no misinterpretation, or misunderstanding, of your Lordship's words, I gave Señor Canovas a memorandum *pro memoriâ* (copy enclosed) of what I had said to him. His Excellency begged me to assure your Lordship that the warm and friendly interest shown by your Lordship and Her Majesty's Government in His Majesty and the Spanish nation would be greatly appreciated by the King and his Government. He trusted that the time was not far distant when I should be authorised to enter into more intimate and formal relations with the Spanish Ministry. 'The friendship of England,' he said, 'was dear and precious to Spain,' and he cordially assented to your Lordship's observation 'that the two nations could never forget the ties which had so long united them in the events of past history; nor could Spain,' he added, 'be otherwise than ever grateful for the many proofs she had received of that friendship.' His Excellency concluded by repeating to me the assurances that he had previously given me, that it was his firm intention to maintain unimpaired the principles of religious freedom.

The other forms vary only in the position given to the date, which is sometimes placed in a separate column, either before or after the names of the correspondents, thus:—

Feb. 3, 1874.   Mr. Layard to   Has represented, &c.
                Foreign Office.

Or thus:—

Mr. Layard to   Feb. 3, 1874.   Has represented, &c.
Foreign Office.

The first form is preferable to the two latter, as it economises space.

It is not very probable, but it is just possible, that a special précis might be required of even such a letter as this. Supposing, for instance, that a question were raised as to the formalities observed by the different Ministers at the Court of Madrid in representing the sentiments of their different nations to the Government of Spain, then such a précis as this would be sufficient:—

Mr. Layard to Foreign Office. Feb. 3, 1874. Called upon the President of the Ministry Regent, expressed the sentiments of H.M. Government, and gave the President a memorandum of what he had said.

In this case the official title of Señor Canovas would be more important than his name, and is therefore used instead of it.

The student who has well mastered all that has gone before will now be able to write the following exercises. He should bear in mind that it is always better to use the words of the original than his own.

The précis may be written with what is called technically a half-margin or a quarter-margin—i.e. a margin on the left side of either half or a quarter of the width of the paper, in which the name of the correspondent and the date should be written. This will give a blank space, except in the case of very short letters, on which memoranda can be written if required.

It is usual in précis to use the name of the Office, Company, or Association instead of the name of the person who signs the letter. In the following exercises 'Foreign Office' may be substituted for 'Lord Tenterden' or 'Earl Granville,' 'Board of Trade' for 'Mr. Farrer,' and 'Salvage Association' for 'Mr. Harper.'

Exercises (E).

1. Make Register Entries, Dockets, or Indices of the following documents, omitting date of receipt except in the cases in which it is given:—

(A)[1]

Lord Tenterden to Mr. Farrer.

FOREIGN OFFICE: April 24, 1875.

SIR,—I am directed by the Earl of Derby to transmit to you a letter from Lloyd's, and I am to request that, in laying it before the Board of Trade, you will state that his Lordship has communicated with Her Majesty's Ambassador at St. Petersburg on that part which relates to the condition of the bar at Kertch; and that if the Board of Trade think that course advisable, he is prepared to make a further representation in regard to that part which refers to grain cargoes.

Lord Derby would, however, be glad to receive the opinion of the Lords of Trade as to the precise form in which any representation on this last point should be made; and I am to observe that this letter from Lloyd's does not contain full information with respect to the regulations stated to be in force at Montreal and New York.

I am, &c.,

(Signed)   TENTERDEN.

(B)

Lord Tenterden to Mr. Harper.

FOREIGN OFFICE: February 14, 1873.

SIR,—I am directed by Earl Granville to state to you that his Lordship has had your letter of the 16th ultimo, respecting the case of the 'Turandot,' under his consideration in communication with the proper Law Advisers of the Crown, and that Her Majesty's Government cannot take any steps in the matter at present—that is to say, until application has been made by the underwriters to, and refused by, the German Government; nor can Her Majesty's Government take any steps at the instance of the Association for the Protection of Commercial

---

[1] In making indices of this and the following letters the first columns should contain the letters (A), (B), &c., as the case may be, instead of numbers.

interests, or of any persons, except those directly interested as underwriters.

I am, &c.,
(Signed)   TENTERDEN.

(C)

Messrs. Vogel, Hagedorn, and Co. to Mr. Austin.

Hong Kong: February 9, 1874.

SIR,—We beg leave to enquire whether there would be any objection to vessels under the Peruvian or Spanish flags proceeding from this port to California, provided that all the rules and regulations now in force are carefully complied with.

Soliciting the favour of an early reply, we have, &c.,

(Signed)   VOGEL, HAGEDORN, & CO.

(D)

Minutes of Proceedings at a Meeting between Sir Hercules Robinson, Thakombau, Maafu, and Tui Thakau, held on board Her Majesty's ship 'Pearl,' at Loma-Loma, on the 2nd of October, 1874.

After some informal remarks, Sir Hercules Robinson said that he supposed that the King had explained to Maafu what had taken place at Levuka, and enquired whether he was of the same mind as he was when he gave the Commodore his letter of the 12th of March.

Maafu replied that he was of the same opinion.

Sir Hercules Robinson then enquired whether Tui Thakau understood the state of affairs, and whether he wished to cede Fiji unconditionally to the Queen.

Tui Thakau replied that he was of the same opinion as the rest of the Chiefs, and that he was thankful for what he had heard.

Sir Hercules Robinson then requested Mr. Wilkinson, the interpreter, to read the Fijian translation of the deed of cession.

Mr. Wilkinson then read the translation of the deed of cession.

The original instrument of cession was then signed by Maafu and Tui Thakau.

The conversation then became informal, and the meeting shortly afterwards closed.

   (Signed)   WALTER HELY-HUTCHINSON.

(E)
Mr. Macdonell to Earl Granville.
(Received July 16.)

MADRID: July 4, 1873.

MY LORD,—With reference to your Lordship's despatch of the 25th ultimo, enclosing copy of a despatch from Acting Consul Crawford on the subject of the liberation of the emancipated slaves in Cuba, I have to inform your Lordship that Señor Suñer y Capdesilla, Minister of Ultramar, stated in the Cortes, on the 28th ultimo, that he purposed presenting to the Chamber a Project of Law for the immediate liberation of the three or four hundred thousand slaves now in that island, adding that it was not possible that he, who had voted the abolition of slavery in Puerto Rico, should now, as a Minister, renounce his former opinion. Furthermore that, as a Federal, he was, so far as it lay in his power, determined that the inhabitants of Cuba shall not only enjoy the liberties which the Republic had bestowed on the Spaniards of the Peninsula, but that he hoped ere long to see that island take its place as one of the independent Cantons of the Spanish Federal Republic.

   I have, &c.,
   (Signed)   H. G. MACDONELL.

(F)
Acting Commissary-Judge Crawford to Earl Granville.
(Received September 29.)

(Extract.)   HAVANA: September 6, 1873.

I have the honour of transmitting herewith to your Lordship a translation of a Project of Law, or Bill, drawn up and proposed to the Spanish Government by the planters here for the emancipation of the negro slaves in the Island of Cuba.

It is proposed to abolish at once the institution of slavery without indemnity to the owners, in place of which they ask for a patronage of ten years over their negroes, during which the negroes are to be treated as 'emancipados,' and are to receive a monthly stipend of two dollars for those between the ages of 12 and 18, three dollars for women, and four dollars for men between the ages of 18 and 60.

All children born since the 17th of September, 1868, and all negroes who have attained or may attain the age of 60 years, are declared free, according to the Law of the 4th of July, 1870.

The patronage is to be transferable, and in cases where there are children under 12 years of age they must be included in the transfer.

The patronage is to cease at the expiry of ten years, by mutual agreement of master and man (which means when the master wishes to give the negro his freedom), by justifiable renunciation of the patron, or through proved abuse, or failure of the patron to comply with his obligations, which are to feed, clothe, and pay his negro, and to furnish him with medical attendance.

At the expiry of the ten years the negroes are to be placed under the patronage of the State (which means that they are to become neither more nor less than 'emancipados'), to be turned over under contract to new or the same masters, and to be rendered bondmen for life.

The planters have added the condition that this Law is not to take effect, and is not to be published in the 'Havana Gazette,' before six months after the insurrection now going on in the island has been officially declared to have terminated.

This Additional Article is sufficient to throw discredit upon the whole scheme; for it is very problematical whether the insurrection will ever end. At any rate, it will be the interest of the slaveholders to keep it alive as long as possible.

The only part of the scheme that really deserves at

tention is the proposal to substitute a patronage, or term of apprenticeship, for an indemnity.

I think that upon that basis a feasible plan of emancipation might be framed to suit the Spanish Government and the slave-owners.

Ten years is much too long a period, and the rate of wages is too small. The final emancipation of the negroes should be fixed at a certain date, after which all 'patronage' should cease.

It would be certainly for the interest of all parties to have this question settled as soon as possible.

(G)

The Chief Justice to the Colonial Secretary.

In re Gardiner's Petitions for Mitigation.

SUPREME COURT: December 6, 1872.

MY DEAR COLONIAL SECRETARY,—I have received a letter (one only of several) from one of Gardiner's sisters, which I think ought to accompany the papers, with a copy of my reply. I therefore enclose both, begging you to submit them with the petitions to his Excellency. Or, if the case is already disposed of, I solicit the favour of your directing the present enclosures to be placed with them.

I have abstained from saying anything about Gardiner's career before his bushranging began, but I can add his previous history if desired. If my sentence on him for horse-stealing, passed at Goulburn, had not been interfered with, he would have had no opportunity of commencing cattle-stealing at Carcoar, or of robbing the gold escort afterwards; for the latter was committed before that sentence had expired.

I am, &c.,

(Signed) ALFRED STEPHEN.

Enclosures.

To his Honour Sir Alfred Stephen.

December 4, 1872.

Sir,—Again I place before you the one earnest wish of my anxious heart, in the hope that you will once more extend your mercy to my dear brother, Francis Christie. Oh, forgive him, for the sake of those who so earnestly plead for him; forgive him, as I hope the Great Judge of all may forgive you and yours when you plead for it. Mercifully grant him his liberation in the colonies, so that his sisters may draw him nearer them and farther from danger. Could you know how we have waited and watched for your answer to our petition—an answer which seems so long delayed—you would have spared us, I believe, some of the anxious suspense; but if the answer be what we could wish, how little will the past misery seem compared to the boon ultimately granted. I know, your Honour, that my brother's sins have been many. I do not wish to think his sentence was unjust, but his punishment has been great and his reformation genuine, and may God grant that it may be your will to again restore my dear brother to freedom. With you his liberation or endless imprisonment rests, so far as earthly power rules; therefore, be that answer what it may, to you, Sir Alfred Stephen, I must look. Be merciful when you would look at the darkest side of this man's character, and forgive me taking the liberty of writing to you as I have done. Trusting that you will pardon my presumption,

I remain, &c.,

(Signed) A. GRIFFITHS.

The Chief Justice has read with deep sympathy the several letters which he has received from Mrs. Griffiths and her sister, and he will forward her letter of yesterday to his Excellency the Governor. The Chief Justice is quite willing to believe all that is represented in Christie's (otherwise Gardiner's) favour; but he feels bound to remember the notoriety of the prisoner's bushranging crimes, and their number, and the frightful evils to which they led, including the deaths of many persons, and the execution of two young men for acts in which Gardiner was the ringleader. Nor can it be forgotten that of the thirty-two years of his sentence one-fourth even has not yet elapsed.

The Chief Justice cannot, therefore, undertake the responsibility of recommending any mitigation in the case. But he does not admit that any such responsibility ought to be cast upon him. It is peculiarly a question for the Governor and Executive Council; and if they should think it right at some future period to remit any portion of the sentence, Sir Alfred Stephen, as an individual, would, for the sake of the Petitioners, be glad to hear of the decision.

SUPREME COURT: December 6, 1872.

(H)

Messrs. Frere and Williamson to the Colonial Office.

November 5, 1874.

MY LORD,—In obedience to the gracious commands of Her Majesty the Queen, contained in Her Commission to us of the 17th day of February, 1872, we have completed our Report upon the treatment of immigrants in Mauritius.

Circumstances with which your Lordship is acquainted have led to unavoidable delay in the completion of the Report; but we have the honour now respectfully to communicate to Her Majesty, through your Lordship, the results of our enquiry, as well as such remarks thereon as we have deemed it our duty to make.

We take this opportunity of expressing through your Lordship our thanks to the Chiefs of the several public Departments in Mauritius, for the assistance and information which we so frequently received from them when we had occasion to call for such, and we may mention the name of Dr. Reid, Chief Medical Officer, who supplied us with much useful information upon the sanitary state of the Island at the time of, and after, the great epidemic of 1867.

Captain Blunt, who, at the time of our arrival, and for some months after, was Acting Inspector-General of Police, was able to render us great assistance both from the position he occupied, and from the knowledge he had gained of the grievances complained of by the old immigrants when serving on the Police Enquiry Commission, which had concluded its labours shortly before our arrival in the Island.

Of the officers holding subordinate positions, we would favourably mention the names of Mr. Daly, District and Stipendiary Magistrate successively of Savanne and Flacq, who gave us much information respecting the working of the Labour Laws, and who, at our request, drew up a paper containing his views upon the procedure of the Stipendiary Courts, of which we have made great use, and which we have appended in full; also of Mr. Robert Mitchell and Mr. W. Seed, who successively filled the post of Assistant-Protector of Immigrants. Of the assistance rendered to us by Mr. Mitchell in compiling complicated tables relating to the amount of work done on sugar estates, we have made frequent mention in our Report. Mr. Seed, who was appointed to succeed him on his departure from the Colony, was employed by us in making enquiries on many special points, and he always discharged his duties with intelligence and trustworthiness. At our desire he drew up a statement explanatory of the numerous forms in use in the Immigration Office, which proved a great assistance to us in the preparation of our chapter on that office.

And, lastly, the name of Mr. Huxtable, of the Procureur-General's Office, who was attached to us, shortly after our arrival, as Assistant to our Secretary, and who continued with us until our departure, during which period he ever discharged his duties to our entire satisfaction.

We have, &c.,

(Signed) W. E. FRERE.
VICTOR A. WILLIAMSON.

2. Make general précis of the same letters.

3. Make special précis of the undermentioned with reference to the points named :—

(A) The regulations at Montreal and New York.

(B) The reason why Lord Derby refused at that time to take any steps.

(D) The witnesses present at the signature of the deed of cession by Maafu.

(E) Cuba.

(F) The Insurrection in Cuba.

(G) The description of crimes committed by Gardiner.

(H) The subordinate officers recommended.

CHAPTER II.

SERIES OF LETTERS.

HITHERTO we have only dealt with single letters; we shall now give some exercises in making a précis of series of letters. In doing this the same principles should be followed as in the case of single letters; but the larger and more important the series, the greater care should be taken both as to fulness and brevity. The whole of a correspondence should be read through carefully before pen is put to paper, so that the whole subject and the relative importance of the facts may be thoroughly grasped, and the writer may be able to make the précis a terse, continuous, and clear narrative of the whole case, purged of all irrelevant and insignificant matter, without redundancy of expression or repetition, a result which it is almost impossible to achieve if an abstract be made of each letter as it is read. If, however, the student find it difficult to retain in his mind the whole of a correspondence, he may make notes of each letter as he goes on, and write his précis from his notes, referring whenever necessary to the correspondence.

There are two forms in which a précis of a series of letters may be made. The contents of each letter may be written separately, or a continuous précis may be made, giving the gist of all the papers in a sequent history, with marginal references to the documents. The following is an example of a series of letters abstracted according to the two methods.

EXAMPLE.

PART OF THE CORRESPONDENCE RELATING TO THE ROYAL COMMISSION OF ENQUIRY INTO THE CONDITION OF THE INDIAN IMMIRGANTS IN MAURITIUS.

No. 1.

The Earl of Kimberley to Governor the Hon. Sir A. Gordon, K.C.M.G.

DOWNING STREET: September 11, 1871.

SIR,—With reference to my despatch of this day's date, commenting on the serious state of affairs which has been brought to light by my enquiries as to the existence of suicide amongst the Indian population of Mauritius, I should wish you to report to me confidentially whether, in your opinion, a Commission of Enquiry into the general condition of the coolies, similar to that which has lately visited British Guiana, would be advisable in the case of Mauritius.

I have, &c.,

(Signed)   KIMBERLEY.

No. 2.

Governor the Hon. Sir A. Gordon, K.C.M G., to the Earl of Kimberley.

(Received December 18.)

MAURITIUS: November 10, 1871.

MY LORD,—In reply to the enquiry contained in your Lordship's despatch of the 11th of September, I have no hesitation in expressing my opinion that an enquiry of the nature contemplated by your Lordship would be of the utmost utility, and indeed, without some such investigation, it is impossible to speak with any confidence as to the position or treatment of the immigrants resident in this island.

2. I have already expressed to your Lordship my belief that, notwithstanding many serious and manifest

defects in the Immigration Laws, the treatment of the immigrants upon estates is, as a rule, kind and just; but, in the absence of anything like efficient inspection or accurate returns, this can only be taken as an impression, nor can it be denied that statements to an opposite effect have been made, not only in the pamphlet recently published by M. de Plevitz (whose assertions, so far as they are made on his own authority alone, cannot be said to carry much weight), but also by other persons of intelligence and character, and that an opinion most unfavourable to the existing system was about three years since publicly expressed, in his place in the Council of Government, by the Colonial Treasurer, a gentleman whose experience of the island is of long standing, and whose integrity is above suspicion.

3. The proceedings in the case of M. de Plevitz, reported in my despatch of the 17th of November, would, moreover, appear to show that an enquiry conducted here by persons connected with the island would be made under pressure of an intimidation which would seriously detract from the value of the conclusions at which they might arrive.

4. It appears to me, therefore, that such a Commission as that which so ably conducted the late enquiry in British Guiana affords the only means of satisfactorily ascertaining the true condition of the labouring population, and of securing the provision of efficient remedies for defects in the existing system of immigration, whether those defects are to be found in the law itself or in its practical administration.

5. I may add that should such a Commission be appointed, it is, in my opinion, absolutely essential that one at least of its members should be well acquainted with the position and treatment of immigrants in the West Indies —a comparison between the two systems being of the utmost importance in arriving at a just impression as to the position of the immigrant here—and should the services of any of the gentlemen who were employed in the conduct of the late enquiry in British Guiana be

available, their presence on the Commission would, I have no doubt, be attended with much advantage.

6. In making, in this confidential form, such a suggestion, your Lordship will not, I hope, think that I have gone beyond the bounds of propriety.

I have, &c.,

(Signed) ARTHUR GORDON.

No. 3.

Governor the Hon. Sir A. Gordon, K.C.M.G., to the Earl of Kimberley.

(Received December 18.)

MAURITIUS: November 17, 1871.

MY LORD,—I have the honour to enclose copies of a Memorial addressed to me by the Chamber of Agriculture on the subject of the pamphlet mentioned in my despatch of this day's date, and of my reply.

2. Your Lordship will observe that, by their second Resolution, the Chamber of Agriculture, in the event of my not adopting a course which, for the reasons given in the speech enclosed in my despatch of this day's date, I have not felt myself justified in pursuing, request the appointment of a Commission to investigate the condition of the Indian immigrants in this Colony, and I beg to commend this request to the serious attention of Her Majesty's Government.

3. That the enquiries of such a Commission might be attended with advantage, cannot, I think, be doubted, and the fact that its appointment has been requested by the agricultural body removes the objections which might have been felt to the adoption of such a measure had it been probable that it would meet with violent opposition or produce general excitement. The only serious objection that can now be urged is the heavy expense which such a measure would undoubtedly entail.

I have, &c.,

(Signed) ARTHUR GORDON.

No. 4.

The Earl of Kimberley to Governor the Hon. Sir A. Gordon, K.C.M.G.

DOWNING STREET: January 19, 1872.

SIR,—In my despatch of the 20th of December I acknowledged the receipt, with other despatches, of your despatch of the 17th of November, enclosing copies of Resolutions adopted by the Chamber of Agriculture of Mauritius, in the second of which it is prayed (in the event of your not seeing reason to take steps to refute the assertions made in a pamphlet published by M. de Plevitz) that 'Her Majesty will name a competent Commission to enquire fully and fairly into all the circumstances, and report on the condition of the Indian labourers employed in the sugar cultivation of the Colony,' and I informed you that I must reserve my opinion as to the necessity for such a Commission until I should have had time to examine fully the communications which I had received from you in connection with this question.

2. I should have been glad if I could have satisfied myself that an enquiry not only involving considerable expense, but tending almost inevitably to arouse feelings of anxiety and excitement, especially among the Indian population, could be dispensed with, and that the amendments in law and practice, which, in my despatch of the 16th of December, I explained to be necessary, and which I felt confident the Legislative Council would readily adopt, might suffice. But after carefully considering the question in all its aspects, I have come to the conclusion that the prayer of the Chamber of Agriculture must be acceded to, and that nothing short of a searching and impartial enquiry into the allegations which have been made, and into all details connected with Indian immigration, would fully answer the twofold purpose of determining what has, in fact, been the condition of the immigrants in the past, and what should be the policy and legislation of the future.

I will therefore proceed to select the most competent persons whom I can procure for this purpose, and will provide for the appointment of the Commission and the opening of the enquiry with as little delay as possible.

I have, &c.,

(Signed) KIMBERLEY.

Précis (Separate).

No. 1. The Earl of Kimberley to the Governor of Mauritius. Sep. 11, 1871.

The existence of suicide among the Indian population of Mauritius. As to whether a Commission of Enquiry into the general condition of coolies in the Colony would be advisable.

No. 2. The Governor of Mauritius to the Earl of Kimberley. Nov. 10, 1871.

The enquiry would be of the utmost utility. Cannot speak confidently as to condition of immigrants without it. Though the Laws relating to Immigration are seriously defective, his impression is that their treatment is, as a rule, good. Opposite statements have, however, been made by persons of intelligence and character, including the Colonial Treasurer, as well as those by M. de Plevitz in his pamphlet, which are not so trustworthy. The proceedings in the case of M. de P. show that the value of an Enquiry by persons connected with the Island would be affected by intimidation. One of the members of the Commission should understand the condition of immigrants in the West Indies, and the employment of gentlemen who conducted the Enquiry in British Guiana is advised.

No. 3. The Governor of Mauritius to the Earl of Kimberley. Nov. 17, 1871.

Encloses Memorial of Chamber of Agriculture, praying Enquiry. As this request removes the fear of violent opposition in the Colony, the only objection is the expense.

No. 4. The Earl of Kimberley to the Governor of Mauritius.
Jan. 19, 1872.

Refers to despatch of December 20, and ack. rec. of No. 3. Regrets but agrees in the necessity for the Enquiry, and will appoint the Commission at once.

Précis (Continuous).

Sep. 11, 1871.

The Earl of Kimberley, in reference to the existence of suicide among the Indian population of Mauritius, asked the Governor to report whether a Commission of Enquiry into the condition of the coolies in the Colony were

Nov. 10, 1871.

desirable. The Governor replied that it would be of the utmost utility, that he could not speak confidently as to the condition of the immigrants, but his impression was that they were treated well as a rule, though the Immigration Laws were seriously defective, and that besides M. de Plevitz (the statements in whose pamphlet were not so trustworthy) persons of intelligence and character, including the Colonial Secretary, had made opposite statements. He added that the proceedings in the case of M. de P. showed that the value of an enquiry held by persons connected with the Island would be affected by intimidation, and suggested that one of the members of the Commission should understand the condition of Immigrants in the West Indies, and that the services of gentlemen who conducted the Enquiry in British Guiana would be of

Nov. 17, 1871.

advantage. A week afterwards the Governor in another despatch forwarded a memorial from the Chamber of Agriculture praying for an Enquiry, in which he stated that, as there was now no fear of violent opposition in the Colony, the only objection was the expense.

Jan. 19 1872. The Earl of Kimberley replied that he would appoint a Commission at once, though he regretted the necessity of it.

Exercises (F).

Make continuous or separate précis of the following series of letters.[1]

(1.) CORRESPONDENCE RESPECTING THE RECOGNITION OF PRINCE ALFONSO AS KING OF SPAIN.

No. 1.

The Earl of Derby to Mr. Layard.

FOREIGN OFFICE: January 5, 1875.

SIR,—I have received your telegraphic despatch of the 31st ultimo, reporting the formation of the Alfonsist Ministry, and that you intend to act in your relations with them in accordance with the instructions you received from Earl Granville on the occasion of the abdication of Prince Amadeo.

In reply I have to acquaint you that Her Majesty's Government approve the course you propose to take.

I am, &c.,

(Signed) DERBY.

---

[1] Should these exercises be found to take an inconveniently long time, they may, for the younger pupils, be shortened in the following manner:—

(1) By omission of Nos. 10, 12, 14, 15, 16.

(2) May be divided into two exercises—(*a*) 1, 2, 3, 4, 5, and (*b*) 6, 7, 8, 9, 10.

(3) By omission of No. 5 and enclosure in No. 6.

(4) May be divided into two exercises—(*a*) 1, 2, 3, 4, 5, 6, 7, and (*b*) 8, 9, 10, 11, 12, 13, 14.

(5) May be similarly divided—(*a*) 1, 2, 3, 4, and (*b*) 5, 6, 7, 8, 9.

No. 2.
The Earl of Derby to Mr. Layard.
(Extract.) FOREIGN OFFICE: January 26, 1875.

In the instructions with which you were furnished on the 5th instant, I confined myself to authorising you to enter into officious relations with the newly constituted Government, and I do not yet feel in a position to instruct you to proceed further in the direction of a formal recognition.

At the same time, while desiring that you should maintain in this respect an attitude of reserve, such as the state of affairs in Spain still requires, Her Majesty's Government are anxious that His Majesty and the Spanish Government should understand that this country is actuated towards Spain by the warmest sentiments of goodwill. The ties which united the two nations in the events of past history cannot, Her Majesty's Government feel confident, be forgotten by either.

It would, therefore, be with unalloyed satisfaction that Her Majesty's Government would welcome the firm establishment of an enlightened, tolerant, and Constitutional Monarchy in Spain, and they hope that His Majesty and his advisers may so take advantage of the present occasion as to realise this object, and re-establish civil order and good administration throughout the Kingdom and its Colonial dependencies.

Her Majesty's Government would wish you to convey this expression of their sentiments to the Government of His Majesty in the manner which may appear to you most suitable.

The policy of Her Majesty's Government is one of non-interference in the internal affairs of foreign States, and they have no intention of departing from it. They cannot, however, but think that the King and his Government may derive support from being acquainted with the view taken of the situation in Spain by the Government of a friendly and disinterested country, and they, therefore, consider that you should lose no fair and becoming opportunity of impressing upon the Spanish Government the vital importance to the King and the people of Spain of maintaining unimpaired the principles of religious freedom.

No. 3.

Sir A. Paget to the Earl of Derby.

(Received January 29.)[1]

ROME: January 26, 1875.

MY LORD,—On leaving Signor Visconti Venosta this morning I met in the anteroom Señor Rances, Marquis of Casa Laiglesias, Minister of the Spanish Republic to this Court, and who has been acting in the same capacity since the proclamation of the Prince of Asturias, who informed me that he had come to announce to Signor Visconti Venosta that he had this morning received a letter for His Majesty the King of Italy from King Alfonso, notifying His Majesty's accession to the throne of Spain.

I have, &c.,

(Signed)   A. PAGET.

No. 4.

Lord A. Loftus to the Earl of Derby.

(Received February 1.)

ST. PETERSBURGH: January 27, 1875.

MY LORD,—Prince Gortchakow informed me yesterday that on the receipt of the official announcement notifying the accession of King Alfonso to the throne of Spain (which was on the road, and was daily expected) the recognition by the Emperor would take place.

I have, &c.,

(Signed)   AUGUSTUS LOFTUS.

---

[1] In the précis, the date of receipt, when given, should be written under the date of the letter.

No. 5.

Lord Odo Russell to the Earl of Derby.

(Received February 1.)

BERLIN: January 26, 1875.

MY LORD,—The Spanish Minister, Count Rascon, had the honour to deliver to the Emperor this day, at a private audience, a letter from King Alfonso, announcing his accession to the throne of Spain.

The Emperor was graciously pleased to say that an early acknowledgment would be sent to the King, together with letters of credence to Count Hatzfeldt, accrediting him as Envoy Extraordinary and Minister Plenipotentiary to His Majesty.

I have, &c.,

(Signed) ODO RUSSELL.

No. 6.

Sir A. Buchanan to the Earl of Derby.

(Received February 1.)

VIENNA: January 28, 1875.

MY LORD,—M. de Mazo, lately accredited as Spanish Minister to this Court by the Government of Marshal Serrano, was received yesterday at a private audience by the Emperor, to deliver a letter to His Majesty from King Alfonso, announcing his accession to the throne.

Letters of credence will, in consequence, be forwarded without further delay to the Austrian Minister at Madrid, accrediting him as the Emperor's Envoy Extraordinary to His Catholic Majesty.

I have, &c.,

(Signed) ANDREW BUCHANAN.

No. 7.
Sir C. Wyke to the Earl of Derby.
(Received February 12.)

COPENHAGEN: February 9, 1875.

MY LORD,—Don Alfonso de Bourbon having by an autograph letter announced to the King of Denmark his accession to the Spanish throne, was replied to yesterday in similar form by the King, who, following the example of most of the other European Sovereigns, has thus acknowledged and recognised that Prince as the legitimate King of Spain.

I have, &c.,
(Signed) CHARLES LENNOX WYKE.

No. 8.
Mr. Morier to the Earl of Derby.
(Received February 14.)

MUNICH: February 4, 1875.

MY LORD,—M. Mazo, the Spanish Minister at Vienna, who is also accredited here, has come to Munich, and been received at an audience by the King for the purpose of notifying to His Majesty the accession of King Alfonso to the throne of Spain.

I have, &c.,
(Signed) R. B. D. MORIER.

No. 9.
Mr. Layard to the Earl of Derby.
(Received February 14.)

(Extract.) MADRID: February 3, 1875.

I called upon Señor Canovas del Castillo yesterday, and communicated to his Excellency the substance of your Lordship's despatch of the 26th ultimo. As your Lordship had left it to me to convey this expression of the sentiments of Her Majesty's Government to that of the King in the manner which might appear to me most suitable, I thought it best to do so to the President of the Ministry-Regent. In order that there should be no misinterpretation or misunderstanding of your Lordship's words, I gave Señor Canovas a Memorandum *pro memoriâ* (copy enclosed) of what I had said to him. His Excellency begged me to assure your Lordship that the warm and friendly interest shown by your Lordship and Her Majesty's Government in His Majesty and the Spanish nation would be greatly appreciated by the King and his Government. He trusted that the time was not far distant when I should be authorised to enter into more intimate and formal relations with the Spanish Ministry. 'The friendship of England,' he said, 'was dear and precious to Spain,' and he cordially assented to your Lordship's observation 'that the two nations could never forget the ties which had so long united them in the events of past history; nor could Spain,' he added, 'be otherwise than ever grateful for the many proofs she had received of that friendship.' His Excellency concluded by repeating to me the assurances that he had previously given me, that it was his firm intention to maintain unimpaired the principles of religious freedom.

Enclosure in No. 9.

Memorandum.

Her Majesty's Government has instructed me to state to his Excellency Señor Canovas del Castillo that England is actuated towards Spain by the warmest sentiments of goodwill, and that the ties which united the two nations in the events of past history cannot, Her Majesty's Government feel confident, be forgotten by either.

It would, therefore, be with unalloyed satisfaction that Her Majesty's Government would welcome the firm establishment of an enlightened, tolerant, and Constitutional Monarchy in Spain, and they hope that His Majesty the King and his advisers may so take advantage of the present occasion as to realise this object and re-establish civil order and good administration throughout the Kingdom and its Colonial dependencies.

The policy of Her Majesty's Government is one of non-interference in the internal affairs of foreign States, and they have no intention of departing from it. But they cannot but consider it entirely consistent with the position of a truly friendly and disinterested Power to impress upon the Spanish Government the vital importance to the King and the people of Spain of maintaining unimpaired the principles of religious freedom.

February 2, 1875.

No. 10.

The Earl of Derby to Mr. Layard.

FOREIGN OFFICE: February 15, 1875.

SIR,—I have received and laid before the Queen your despatch of the 3rd instant, and I have to state to you in reply that Her Majesty's Government approve your having communicated to Señor Canovas del Castillo the substance of my despatch of the 26th ultimo, by which you were informed of the sentiments entertained by Her Majesty's Government towards the Government of Don Alfonso.

I am, &c.,

(Signed)   DERBY.

No. 11.

The Earl of Derby to Mr. Layard.

FOREIGN OFFICE: February 15, 1875.

SIR,—I transmit to you a letter which the Queen has been pleased to address to the King of Spain accrediting you to His Majesty in the character of her Envoy Extraordinary and Minister Plenipotentiary, and I am to desire that you will deliver the same in the usual form accompanied by suitable compliments in Her Majesty's name upon his accession to the throne.

A copy of your letter of credence is also enclosed.

I am, &c.,

(Signed)   DERBY

No. 12.
Circular addressed to Her Majesty's Ministers at European Courts.

FOREIGN OFFICE: February 15, 1875.

MY LORD—SIR,—I have to inform you that Her Majesty's credentials will this day be forwarded to Mr. Austen Henry Layard, accrediting him Her Majesty's Envoy Extraordinary and Minister Plenipotentiary at the Court of His Majesty King Alfonso XII.

I am, &c.,
(Signed)   DERBY.

No. 13.
Mr. Fenton to the Earl of Derby.
(Received February 17.)

(Extract.)   THE HAGUE: February 15, 1875.

With reference to my despatch of the 3rd instant, I have the honour to inform your Lordship that I learn from the Netherlands Minister for Foreign Affairs that the King of the Netherlands has addressed a letter to King Alfonso, in reply to that lately received from him, acknowledging His Majesty as King of Spain.

No. 14.
The Earl of Derby to Mr. Layard.

FOREIGN OFFICE: February 20, 1875.

SIR,—I have received the Queen's commands to desire that, in presenting to the King of Spain the credentials with which you have been furnished, accrediting you to His Majesty, you will offer to him the Queen's sincere congratulations on his accession to the throne of Spain, and Her Majesty's warm wishes for his happiness and prosperity.

The Queen entertains the earnest hope that His Majesty's reign will be characterised by an enlightened, constitutional, and tolerant policy, such as may tend to promote the welfare of the country over which he has been called upon to preside.

I am, &c.,

(Signed) DERBY.

No. 15.

Mr. Layard to the Earl of Derby.

(Received March 6.)

MADRID: February 27, 1875.

MY LORD,—Accompanied by the members of Her Majesty's Legation, I had to-day the honour of being received by the King for the purpose of delivering Her Majesty's letter of congratulation on his accession to the throne, and the letter accrediting me as Her Majesty's Envoy Extraordinary and Minister Plenipotentiary to this Court, and I beg to transmit to your Lordship herewith copy of my address to His Majesty, as well as of his reply, with a translation thereof.

I have, &c.,

(Signed) A. H. LAYARD.

Enclosure 1 in No. 15.

Mr. Layard's Address to the King of Spain.

SIR,—I have the honour to deliver to your Majesty the answer of the Queen, my gracious Sovereign, to the letter of your Majesty, announcing your Majesty's accession to the throne, and at the same time a letter from Her Majesty, by which she is pleased to accredit me in the character of her Envoy Extraordinary and Minister Plenipotentiary.

I am specially commanded by Her Majesty to offer to your Majesty her sincere congratulations and her warm wishes for your Majesty's happiness and prosperity, and to express to your Majesty her hopes that your Majesty's reign will be marked by a constitutional, enlightened, and tolerant policy, such as may tend to promote the welfare of Spain.

It is the earnest desire of the Queen and her people that the friendly relations which have so long and so happily subsisted between Spain and England should be maintained and improved. I trust that, in my endeavours to contribute to this object, I shall deserve and obtain your Majesty's confidence and support.

Enclosure 2 in No. 15.

The King of Spain's Reply to Mr. Layard.

(Translation.)

M. LE MINISTRE,—I receive with true pleasure the answer of your august Sovereign to the communication of my accession to the throne, and the letter in which she accredits you as her Envoy Extraordinary and Minister Plenipotentiary.

The felicitation which you are charged to present to me on the part of Her Britannic Majesty, and her hope that my efforts will be principally directed to promote the well-being of my country by the means best fitted to that end, are of great value to me.

I beg you, M. le Ministre, to transmit to Her Majesty the Queen my profound gratitude for her benevolent sentiments, which I have great pleasure in reciprocating by my fervent wishes for her constant happiness and for that of her people, and assure her that my desire and that of Spain to preserve and draw closer the relations of cordial friendship happily and long existing with England is not less lively.

I do not doubt that you will contribute to that laudable object with your zeal and distinguished qualities, and for that purpose you will always find in me the benevolent support for which you reasonably ('fundadamente') hope.

No. 16.
The Earl of Derby to Mr. Layard.

FOREIGN OFFICE: March 10, 1875.

SIR,—I have received and laid before the Queen your despatch of the 27th ultimo, in which you report your reception by the King of Spain, and your delivery to His Majesty of the Queen's letter of congratulation on his accession to the throne, and of the letter accrediting you as Her Majesty's Envoy Extraordinary and Minister Plenipotentiary at the Court of Spain.

I have to state to you that Her Majesty's Government approve your address to His Majesty the King on the occasion in question, copy of which is enclosed in your above-mentioned despatch.

I am, &c.,
(Signed)   DERBY.

(2.) CORRESPONDENCE RESPECTING THE MACAO COOLIE TRADE, 1874–75.

No. 1.
Mr. Herbert to Lord Tenterden.
(Received April 20.)

DOWNING STREET: April 20, 1874.

SIR,—I am directed by the Earl of Carnarvon to transmit to you, for the consideration of the Earl of Derby, two despatches lately received from Sir Arthur Kennedy, reporting the refusal of the Governor to allow Peruvian and Spanish vessels to embark free Chinese emigrants at the port of Hong Kong.

The Governor has full power to grant or withhold his license; and in stating this to Lord Derby, I am to request that you will inform his Lordship that, in Lord Carnarvon's opinion, Sir Arthur Kennedy was perfectly right in the policy adopted on the present occasion; and his Lordship proposes, with Lord Derby's concurrence, to approve of the manner in which the Governor has exercised the discretion entrusted to him by the law.

I am, &c.,

(Signed) ROBERT G. W. HERBERT.

No. 2.

Lord Tenterden to Mr. Herbert.

FOREIGN OFFICE: April 23, 1874.

SIR,—I am directed by the Earl of Derby to acknowledge the receipt of your letter of the 20th instant in regard to the refusal of the Governor of Hong Kong to allow Peruvian and Spanish vessels to embark free Chinese emigrants, and I am to request that you will state to the Earl of Carnarvon that Lord Derby fully concurs in his Lordship's proposal to approve Sir A. Kennedy's proceedings on the occasion in question.

I am, &c.,

(Signed) TENTERDEN.

No. 3.

Lord Odo Russell to the Earl of Derby.

(Received April 27.)

BERLIN: April 20, 1874.

MY LORD,—In a discussion in the Reichstag on the 18th of April on the Supplementary Budget of 1874, Deputy Kapp asked President Delbrück whether he had official intelligence that German citizens and merchants had engaged in the coolie trade between Macao and Callao, under the Peruvian flag, and were still engaged therein, that German captains of ships have forwarded coolies from the eastern coasts of Asia to Peru, and what steps the Imperial Chancery has taken to stop such offences.

President Delbrück replied, that it had been reported in the newspapers that a 'German firm in Hong Kong had been shipping coolies, and that very sad things had occurred. This appeared in a Blue Book of the English Parliament. It was found, on further investigation, that if there had been any infraction of the law, it had happened under English jurisdiction at Hong Kong, and we promised our co-operation in any proceedings which might be taken. The English lawyers were, however, of opinion that there was no ground for action, so that neither could there be any action on our part. The legal position of the coolie trade is as follows :—

'The shipment of coolies commenced when the Slave Trade ceased. For a long time the Chinese Government troubled themselves little about the subject. A later attempt to mend matters did not succeed; and the subject was first taken up again in earnest by the Treaties of Peace concluded by Great Britain and France with China in 1860. These recognised the right of emigration to Chinese; but it was wished to frame regulations for preventing this right from being misused in the engaging, or by the maltreatment, of emigrants. In 1866 regulations were agreed upon for emigration from China, which appear to me to be entirely suitable. They were communicated to all the Powers, and forthwith published in China as a law of the country. One Article, however, stipulated that a Chinese might not engage himself before emigrating for longer than five years; besides, the Chinese was to be brought back gratis by the Agent under certain conditions. France and England demanded an alteration of these Articles, but China refused. The Regulations therefore exist, and regulate the case for the German flag. There is only one omission, which is, that as far as relates to the disposition and maintenance of coolies, they are placed under the rules of the flag under which the ship sails. This is the case with the above-mentioned Articles. Now, as we have no legal regulations in these matters, the German Consulates have published such in order to render possible the transport of coolies on our ships. I can only say that the Consulates, according to the instructions given to them and the Legation at Peking, will take strict care that the German flag shall not be misused.'

I have, &c.,

(Signed) ODO RUSSELL.

No. 4.

The Earl of Derby to Sir C. Murray.

FOREIGN OFFICE: April 30, 1874.

SIR,—I enclose for your information, and for such enquiries as you may be able to make into the matter, an extract from a despatch from Her Majesty's Consul-General in the Havana, mentioning a report that the coolie traffic from Macao is being resumed under the name of free emigration.

I am, &c.,

(Signed) DERBY.

No. 5.

Sir B. Robertson to Lord Tenterden.

(Received May 11.)

CANTON: March 31, 1874.

MY LORD,—I have the honour to enclose a copy of a despatch, and its enclosures I have sent to Her Majesty's Minister at Peking. They enclose a proclamation by the Viceroy and Governor of these Provinces, announcing the extinction of the coolie traffic at Macao.

I have, &c.,

(Signed) B. ROBERTSON.

No. 6.

The Earl of Derby to Mr. Cobbold.

FOREIGN OFFICE: October 10, 1874.

SIR,—I transmit to you an extract of a despatch from Her Majesty's Consul-General at the Havana, relative to negotiations which he understands are likely to be made at Lisbon with a view to reopening the coolie trade from Macao.

You will, of course, not fail to report to me anything that may come to your knowledge with regard to the alleged negotiations.

I am, &c.,

(Signed) DERBY.

No. 7.

Mr. Cobbold to the Earl of Derby.

(Received October 15.)

LISBON: October 16, 1874.

MY LORD,—I have taken occasion to bring to the notice of the Portuguese Minister for Foreign Affairs the subject of the Macao Coolie Traffic, more especially that under the denomination of 'free emigration.' I did not fail to point out to his Excellency the deep interest evinced by Her Majesty's Government in the total suppression of this traffic, not alone in the cause of humanity, but in the very interests of civilisation; and I clearly stated it as the opinion of my Government that the traffic in question, under whatever head, would never be entirely done away with unless the Portuguese Government were prepared to enforce to its utmost extent their Decree of March 1873.

Senhor Corvo, in reply, said that he considered this question as one of the past, as regards Portugal; he assured me that, in March of this year, he even telegraphed to the Governor of Macao not to allow free emigration, as he feared it might serve as a cloak to the old traffic; and the advices received from that Colony state that all the vessels now leaving Macao do so in ballast.

The new Governor of Macao is appointed to leave for his post about the middle of this month, and he takes with him positive instructions to carry out all the engagements of Portugal with regard to the suppression of the coolie traffic, coupled with the strictest orders not even to allow free emigration.

His Excellency further stated that a contemplated Treaty between Portugal and Peru has not yet been ratified owing to the question of coolie emigration, and that he considers the negotiations at an end, inasmuch as he has written to the Portuguese Consul at Lima that he may come home on leave.

I have, &c.,

(Signed)   T. CLEMENT COBBOLD.

No. 8.
The Earl of Derby to Mr. Cobbold.

FOREIGN OFFICE: October 19, 1874.

SIR,—I have to instruct you to express to the Portuguese Minister for Foreign Affairs the satisfaction with which Her Majesty's Government have received his Excellency's assurances of the determination of the Portuguese Government not to allow a revival of the Macao Coolie Traffic in any form, as reported in your despatch of the 6th instant.

I am, &c.,

(Signed)   DERBY.

No. 9.
The Earl of Derby to Mr. Cobbold.

FOREIGN OFFICE: March 2, 1875.

SIR,—With reference to my despatch of the 12th of October, I transmit to you copies of despatches from Her Majesty's Consul at Canton, and from the Governor of Hong Kong.

You will see from these despatches that fears are entertained both by Sir Brooke Robertson and by Sir Arthur Kennedy, that influential persons interested in the coolie traffic may take advantage of the arrival at Macao of the new Governor, Senhor d'Avila, in order to make a strong effort to bring about a revival of that traffic.

I have to instruct you to communicate the substance of the enclosed despatches to the Portuguese Minister for Foreign Affairs.

In doing so you will state that the positive assurances given to you by his Excellency, as reported in your despatch of the 6th of October, have fully satisfied Her Majesty's Government of the sincere desire of the Portuguese Government not to allow the coolie traffic from Macao to be resumed in any shape; and Her Majesty's Government, therefore, feel sure that the Portuguese Government will be glad to be informed of the efforts that are likely to be made for its renewal, in order that they may take prompt measures to prevent the success of those efforts.

You will add that, in view of the fact stated by Sir Arthur Kennedy, that the suspension of the Regulations for the coolie traffic expires on the 1st of April, Her Majesty's Government urges upon the Government of His Most Faithful Majesty the propriety of sending instructions upon this subject at once by telegraph to the Government of Macao.

I am, &c.,

(Signed)   DERBY.

No. 10.
Mr. Cobbold to the Earl of Derby.
(Received April 22.)

LISBON: March 22, 1875.

MY LORD,—With reference to your despatch of the 2nd instant, I have the honour to enclose to your Lordship herewith translation of a note, dated the 19th instant, from the Portuguese Minister for Foreign Affairs, in which his Excellency states that the new Governor of Macao and Timor has been furnished with instructions to prohibit, until further orders, emigration under contract as well as all free emigration.

I have, &c.,

(Signed)   T. CLEMENT COBBOLD.

(3.) A COPY OF CORRESPONDENCE BETWEEN THE BOARD OF TRADE AND FOREIGN OFFICE AND THE COMMITTEE OF LLOYD'S ON THE SUBJECT OF GRAIN CARGOES.

No. 1.

The Secretary of Lloyd's to Lord Tenterden.

(Received April 20.)

LLOYD'S: April 19, 1875.

SIR,—I am directed by the Committee of Lloyd's to inform you that it has been reported to the Committee that measures for deepening the bar at Kertch have been instituted by the Government of His Majesty the Emperor of Russia, and that the works proceed only with great delays.

I am directed further to point out to you that, in consequence of want of water on that bar, considerable damage and loss is incurred by both ships and cargoes, and consequently much loss is sustained by merchants and underwriters interested in the trade of the Azov. I am, therefore, to request you to be good enough to bring these matters under the notice of the Earl of Derby, in order that his Lordship may allow such steps to be taken as he may deem advisable to draw the attention of the Russian Government to the necessity for the rapid completion of the works for deepening the bar at Kertch.

I am further directed by the Committee of Lloyd's to bring under your notice the great saving of life and property that would, without doubt, be effected by an adoption at the grain-loading ports in the Black Sea of some regulations with reference to the stowage of grain cargoes similar to those now enforced at Montreal and also at New York. From the semi-fluid character of these cargoes great danger is experienced in heavy weather from their constant displacement by the motion of the vessel, if not adequately secured. Even under the most favourable circumstances they always settle into a much smaller space than that which is originally occupied when they are first loaded, and this also has a tendency to render useless shifting boards and other safeguards, unless very carefully provided.

No less than five steamers from the Black Sea foundered during the months of November, December, and January, while a sixth was abandoned from the same cause, but subsequently recovered. The number of lives lost on board these vessels can hardly be estimated at less than 140. It is further to be noted that one of these five, during the winter of 1873, brought a cargo of like quantity across the Atlantic in perfect safety through equally severe weather. Her captain attributed his safety upon this voyage to the fact of one-third of his cargo having been stowed in bags upon the top of the remaining portion in bulk, while, when coming lately from the Black Sea, this precaution was omitted, and the loss of twenty-eight lives would appear to have been the consequence. Even on so short a voyage as from Antwerp to London seven lives, as well as the ship and cargo, were lately lost from the shifting of a cargo of linseed on board a steamer called the 'Princess.' The Committee of Lloyd's believe that enquiries of all who are conversant with this subject will confirm the view they are now taking, and which has been most forcibly brought under their notice by the very marked effect upon the safety of steamers bringing grain from Montreal to New York, owing to the punctual enforcement of the regulations mentioned above since the disastrous winter of 1872–73.

In addition to the painful argument furnished by the less of so many lives every winter from this cause, you will observe that the loss of so much property must have a tendency to raise both freights and premiums, and by this increase of the cost of importation tell against the welfare of the great Empire of Russia in competition with other grain-exporting countries. It thus becomes greatly the interest of the Government of that country to enforce rules that have been found in practice so beneficial, even if the lives directly affected thereby should be mainly those of our own countrymen.

I am, &c.,

(Signed)   H. M. HOZIER, *Secretary.*

No. 2.
Lord Tenterden to Mr. Farrer.

FOREIGN OFFICE: April 24, 1875.

SIR,—I am directed by the Earl of Derby to transmit to you a letter from Lloyd's, and I am to request that, in laying it before the Board of Trade, you will state that his Lordship has communicated with Her Majesty's Ambassador at St. Petersburg on that part which relates to the condition of the bar at Kertch; and that if the Board of Trade think that course advisable, he is prepared to make a further representation in regard to that part which refers to grain cargoes.

Lord Derby would, however, be glad to receive the opinion of the Lords of Trade as to the precise form in which any representation on this last point should be made; and I am to observe that this letter from Lloyd's does not contain full information with respect to the regulations stated to be in force at Montreal and New York.

I am, &c.,

(Signed) TENTERDEN.

No. 3.
Lord Tenterden to the Secretary of Lloyd's.

FOREIGN OFFICE: April 24, 1875.

SIR,—I am directed by the Earl of Derby to acknowledge the receipt of your letter of the 20th instant, and I am to state to you in reply, for the information of the Committee of Lloyd's, that the representations therein made relative to the condition of the bar at Kertch and grain cargoes from Russian ports in the Black Sea are receiving his Lordship's attention.

I am, &c.,

(Signed) TENTERDEN.

No. 4.

Mr. Farrer to Lord Tenterden.

(Received July 13.)

BOARD OF TRADE, WHITEHALL GARDENS: July 12, 1875.

MY LORD,—I am directed by the Board of Trade to acknowledge the receipt of your letter of the 24th of April last, transmitting a letter from Lloyd's relating (1) to the condition of the bar at Kertch, and (2) to the need for some regulations for the stowage of grain cargoes at ports in the Black Sea similar to those that are in force at Montreal and New York.

The latter of these two subjects is, no doubt, one of very serious importance as regards the safety both of lives and property, but the Board of Trade hesitate to advise his Lordship to make a representation on the subject to the Russian Government for the following reasons:—

1. They have not yet succeeded in obtaining copies of the rules in force at Montreal and New York, and it is very doubtful whether rules made for one port would be applicable or advisable at another.

2. A dangerous precedent might be established if a foreign Government were invited to legislate or make regulations for British shipping. Such regulations might be injudicious in themselves, whilst their application by the foreign authorities might be unjust; and remonstrances against their abuse would lack force from their having been made at the request of Her Majesty's Government.

3. Any general regulations at a foreign port would affect ships of other nations, and any special regulations for British ships might act injuriously to British commerce.

4. Underwriters and shipowners might do much to effect the desired object without Government interference.

Under these circumstances the Board are in communication with Lloyd's to see whether steps cannot be taken to secure the adoption of proper rules without applying for the compulsory interference of the Russian Government.

I have, &c.,
(Signed) T. H. FARRER.

No. 5.

Lord Tenterden to the Secretary of Lloyd's.

FOREIGN OFFICE: July 17, 1875.

SIR,—With reference to the letter from this Office of the 24th of April last, I am directed by the Earl of Derby to state to you, for the information of the Committee of Lloyd's, that his Lordship has considered, in consultation with the Lords of Trade, the questions adverted to in your letter of the 20th of April, respecting the condition of the bar at Kertch, and the need for some regulations for the stowage of grain cargoes at ports in the Black Sea similar to those that are in force at Montreal and New York.

I am now to observe that the latter of these two subjects is, no doubt, one of very serious importance as regards the safety both of lives and property, but Lord Derby does not deem it advisable to make a representation on the subject to the Russian Government for the following reasons:—

1. This Office is not yet in possession of copies of the rules in force in Montreal and New York, and it is very doubtful whether rules made for one port would be applicable or advisable at another.

2. A dangerous precedent might be established if a foreign Government were invited to legislate or make regulations for British shipping. Such regulations might be injudicious in themselves, whilst their application by the foreign authorities might be unjust, and remonstrances against their abuse would lack force from the regulations having been made at the request of Her Majesty's Government.

3. Any general regulations at a foreign port would

affect ships of other nations, and any special regulations for British ships might act injuriously to British commerce.

4. It appears to Lord Derby that underwriters and shipowners might do much to effect the desired object without Government interference.

I am, in conclusion, to state that Lord Derby understands that the Board of Trade are in communication with the Committee of Lloyd's, with a view to ascertain whether steps cannot be taken to secure the adoption of proper rules without applying for the compulsory interference of the Russian Government.

I am, &c.,

(Signed)   TENTERDEN.

No. 6.

The Secretary of Lloyd's to Lord Tenterden.

(Received July 22.)

LLOYD'S: July 21, 1875.

MY LORD, — I am directed by the Committee of Lloyd's to acknowledge with thanks the receipt of your letter of the 17th instant.

I have only to remark, in reply, that it was not the intention of the Committee of Lloyd's to suggest a special law for British vessels loading at Russian ports that was not applicable to those of other nations, but a universal regulation which might be applicable to vessels of all flags alike.

The paragraph 4 of your letter is that which the Committee of Lloyd's is most concerned to answer, and perhaps I may possibly place before your Lordship the opinion of the Committee by enclosing a copy of a letter which has been written to the Board of Trade in reply to the communication from that Department upon the same subject, alluded to in your Lordship's letter of the 17th instant.

I have, &c.,

(Signed)   H. M. HOZIER, *Secretary.*

Enclosure in No. 6.

The Secretary of Lloyd's to the Assistant-Secretary to the Board of Trade.

LLOYD'S: July 21, 1875.

SIR,—I have to acknowledge your letter of the 10th of July (replying to mine of the 19th of April addressed to the Foreign Office and referred to your Department) suggesting that instead of claiming the interference of the Russian Government to control the stowage of grain cargoes shipped from the Black Sea, the owners and underwriters should be the persons by whom a better state of loading should be enforced.

The Committee would probably not have gone further into this question had it not been for the concluding paragraph of your letter, desiring their opinion upon the practicability of their action conducing to a better system; and upon this subject they are glad to have an opportunity of saying a few words, as it seems to them that there is much misconception about it.

The province of underwriters is not to lead, but to follow, the course of trade; for the machinery by which commerce is carried on is independent of their control or consent; nor are the interests represented by the Committee really concerned in the matter, for whatever the risks of any special trade may be, proportionately to those risks is the payment for insurance ultimately regulated.

It is possible that the interesting letter from the Consul-General at New York of the 24th of June, 1875, sent here from your Department, may have led to a belief that it is within the power of underwriters to regulate the loading of cargoes of the same description as those, the subject of this correspondence. But I beg to point out to you that the control the New York underwriters possess is limited to those ships the insurance of which is offered to their particular associated offices of the Board of Underwriters, while at Montreal, where Government interference prevails, the rules are absolute and general. Further, what may be possible by association in a limited area of business becomes impracticable when that area is greatly extended ; and such a combination in England would simply result in transferring the market for insurance to other countries.

The Committee indeed entertain doubts whether such a power of control among underwriters (though apparently useful in the present instance) would always be for the advantage of commerce.

The Committee, fearing to go at greater length into this question at this moment, have intended to show very shortly that underwriters do not possess the power, and then that they have no direct interest in urging the point referred to in their letter of the 19th of April, and that they were moved only by a desire to bring authority to bear on a custom of trade that led directly to lamentable loss of life and inevitable destruction of property.

They consider these subjects as directly coming under the legitimate interference of Governments, and that by them alone they can be effectually dealt with ; and the Committee would be glad if you could decide to share these views, and return the letter to the Foreign Office backed with the influence of your opinion.

I am, &c.,

(Signed)   HENRY M. HOZIER, *Secretary.*

No. 7.

Lord Tenterden to the Secretary to Lloyd's.

FOREIGN OFFICE : July 23, 1875.

SIR,—I am directed by the Earl of Derby to acknowledge the receipt of your letter of the 21st instant, containing further observations on the part of the Committee of Lloyd's with respect to the regulations for loading vessels at Russian ports.

I am, &c.,

(Signed)   TENTERDEN.

(4.) CORRESPONDENCE RESPECTING THE GERMAN VESSEL 'TURANDOT,' CAPTURED BY A FRENCH CRUISER DURING THE FRANCO-GERMAN WAR.

No. 1.

Messrs. Smith, Sundius, and Co. to Earl Granville.

(Received March 3.)

33 GRACECHURCH STREET, LONDON, E.C: March 1, 1873.

MY LORD,—We are insurance brokers in this city.

During the late war between France and Germany we effected insurances for 6,400*l*. upon the following goods laden on board the German ship 'Turandot,' Captain Meinert, from Hamburg, bound to Hong Kong, viz. :—

E S & C	25 rolls of wire rope.
F P	500 cases window glass.
[L] F W E L }	250 steel tubes.
E S & C	50 casks beef.
Adler Reff. Harzblei }	1,079 blocks of lead.
	1,000 bundles of iron.
	600 ditto.
F O K	1 case of matches.
B F	346 cases ditto.
E S & C	81 cases of glassware.

The said ship was captured and taken to Saigon by the French cruiser 'Segond;' the above goods were sold there and realised 104,047*f*. 15*c*.

The account sales and money for the proceeds were received by the Director of Prizes in Paris on or about the 2nd of January, 1872.

Our agent, M. A. Châteauneuf Jeune, residing at 8 Boulevard Montmartre, Paris, has since made many applications for payment of said sum of 104,047*f*. 15*c*.

He was told that owing to various interests being mixed up and accounted for in one sum, the French Court of Prizes had proposed to the Reichskanzler in Berlin to pay over the proceeds to him for distribution among the interested.

Afterwards he was informed by the Court of Prizes in Paris that the Reichskanzler had declined, or was unable, to make the distribution.

We have, when in Paris (through the courtesy of M. Bourdin at the Prize Court), seen the account sales, and found the proceeds of sale of our above parcels of goods separately enumerated and distinctly defined.

Wherefore we pray that your Lordship will be so good as to direct our Ambassador at Paris to see the authorities there and procure a prompt payment of the proceeds of sale to our said agent, M. Châteauneuf, unless, indeed, the French Government prefer to pay the sum to our Ambassador for transmission to your Lordship and for payment by you to the interested.

We are, &c.,

(Signed)   SMITH, SUNDIUS, & Co.

No. 2.

Viscount Enfield to Messrs. Smith, Sundius, & Co.

FOREIGN OFFICE: March 11, 1873.

GENTLEMEN,—In reply to your letter of the 1st instant, I am directed by Earl Granville to inform you that his Lordship has instructed Her Majesty's Ambassador at Paris to make enquiry concerning your claim on the French Prize Court for the proceeds of the sale of certain goods shipped on board the German vessel 'Turandot,' which you had insured before her capture by a French cruiser; and his Excellency has been instructed to give you such assistance in prosecuting your claim as he can properly afford.

I am, &c.,

(Signed)   ENFIELD.

No. 3.

Earl Granville to Lord Lyons.

FOREIGN OFFICE: March 11, 1873.

MY LORD,—I transmit to your Excellency a copy of a letter from Messrs. Smith, Sundius, and Co., a firm who claim from the French Prize Court the proceeds of the sale of certain goods stowed on board the German ship 'Turandot' when she was captured during the late war by a French cruiser, which goods the firm had insured; and I am to request your Excellency to be so good as to enquire into this matter, and to give to the firm such assistance in pursuing the claim in question as you can properly afford, reporting to me the steps, if any, which your Excellency may feel justified in taking in this matter.

I am, &c.,

(Signed) GRANVILLE.

No. 4.

Lord Lyons to Earl Granville.

(Received March 19, 1873.)

PARIS: March 17, 1873.

MY LORD,—I had yesterday the honour to receive your Lordship's despatch of the 11th instant, enclosing a copy of a letter from Messrs. Smith and Sundius praying your Lordship to direct me to see the French authorities here and procure a prompt payment to their agents of a sum of money claimed by them in a Prize Case, unless, indeed, the French Government prefer to pay the sum to me for transmission to your Lordship, and for payment by you to the interested.

The claim appears to arise from an insurance effected by Messrs. Smith and Sundius on goods on board a German ship, the 'Turandot,' which was captured and taken into Saigon by a French cruiser; and it is stated that the goods in question were sold, and the proceeds received by the Director of Prizes in Paris, on or about the 2nd of January, 1872.

Payment appears to have been delayed; but Messrs. Smith and Sundius's letter does not show with sufficient precision what, if any, steps they have taken to establish their claim before the Prize Court, and obtain payment for it in the regular course. They merely say that their agent at Paris has made many applications for payment.

The general instructions given to Her Majesty's Embassy are, not to interfere in Prize Cases, and it appears to me that I should not be justified, as at present advised, in departing from those instructions. Your Lordship will probably think that before demanding payment of the money from the French Government, or even so far intervening in the case as to call upon the Government to furnish us with information respecting it, we should be supplied by the claimants with *primâ facie* evidence that our interference would be justifiable and necessary. In fact, according to the ordinary principle, the claimants should show that they have exhausted the legal means at their disposal, and that there has been such a delay or denial of justice as would warrant Her Majesty's Government in demanding redress for them, as a question between Government and Government.

I am far from wishing to act over scrupulously upon this principle, but I do not think Messrs. Smith and Sundius have in their letter made their case sufficiently clear to warrant me in taking any steps concerning it without further information.

I wait, therefore, for further instructions from your Lordship.

I have, &c.,
(Signed) LYONS.

No. 5.

Mr. Hammond to Messrs. Smith, Sundius, and Co.

FOREIGN OFFICE: March 27, 1873.

GENTLEMEN,—With reference to Lord Enfield's letter of the 11th instant, respecting your claim against the

French Prize Courts, on account of the sale of certain goods forming part of the cargo of the German vessel 'Turandot' when she was captured by a French cruiser during the late war, I am directed to inform you that a despatch has been received from Her Majesty's Ambassador at Paris, in which his Excellency states that your letter does not show with sufficient precision what, if any, steps have been taken to establish your claim before the Prize Court, and obtain judgment of it in the regular course, but that you refer only to your agent at Paris having made many applications for payment.

It is right that you should be aware that it is no part of the duty of Her Majesty's Embassies or Legations abroad to interfere, under ordinary circumstances, in cases before Prize Courts, and in the present instance Her Majesty's Ambassador would not be justified on the information you have as yet furnished in regard to your claim in departing from this principle.

Before, therefore, Lord Granville can instruct Lord Lyons to make any application to the French Government on your behalf, it will be necessary that you should supply *primâ facie* evidence that such interference would be justifiable and necessary, which would not, under ordinary circumstances, be the case, unless you can show that you have exhausted the legal means at your disposal, and that there has been such a delay or denial of justice as would warrant the intervention of Her Majesty's Embassy in your behalf.

I am, &c.,

(Signed)   E. HAMMOND.

No. 6.

Messrs. Smith, Sundius, and Co. to Earl Granville.

(Received November 12.)

33 GRACECHURCH STREET, LONDON, E.C.: November 8, 1873.

MY LORD,—We duly received your Lordship's favour of the 27th of March. Since which we have been at Paris, and have satisfied ourselves that 242,000*f.* have been sent to the Minister of Foreign Affairs at Berlin by the Prize Court at Paris for division among those concerned in the proceeds of the sale of the ship 'Turandot' and her cargo.

We have therefore sought, through the German Consul here, repayment of the sum of 104,047f., which is shown to be due to the underwriters (whom we represent) in respect of certain items referred to in our letter to your Lordship dated the 1st of March last, but are informed by him that our application must be addressed to the Imperial German Ministry for Foreign Affairs, through the medium of your Lordship and Her Majesty's Ambassador at Berlin. We therefore beg leave to avail ourselves of the permission given us in your Lordship's letter of the 27th of March (having exhausted all means at our disposal), to beg the favour of your communicating with Mr. Odo Russell at Berlin, asking him to communicate with the Imperial Foreign Office, and obtain for us the payment of the equivalent of said sum of 104,047f.

We are, &c.,

(Signed) SMITH, SUNDIUS, & Co.

No. 7.

Viscount Enfield to Messrs. Smith, Sundius, and Co.

FOREIGN OFFICE: November 21, 1873.

GENTLEMEN,—I am directed by Earl Granville to acknowledge the receipt of your letter of the 8th instant, requesting the intervention of Her Majesty's Representative at Berlin in obtaining for you, from the German Government, the payment of a sum which you claim as part of the proceeds of the sale of the ship 'Turandot' during the late Franco-German war, the proceeds of that sale having, you state, been sent to Berlin by the French Prize Court for division among those concerned.

I am to state to you, in reply, that Lord Granville does not consider that you have yet established any claim for the formal intervention of Her Majesty's Government. You do not appear to have exhausted all the legal means at your disposal for obtaining payment of your claim from the German Government, nor have you shown that there has been any such delay or denial of justice as would alone warrant the interference of Her Majesty's Ambassador.

I am, &c.,
(Signed)   ENFIELD.

No. 8.

Messrs. Smith, Sundius, and Co. to the Earl of Derby.

(Received September 17.)

33 GRACECHURCH STREET, LONDON: September 16, 1874.

MY LORD,—We beg your Lordship's reference to your predecessor's letter to us of the 21st of November, 1873, in reference to which we subjoin copy of letter from the Reichskanzler's office to Dr. Albert Wolffson, our solicitor at Hamburg, proving that we have exhausted all legal means at our disposal for obtaining payment of our claim from the German Government for the handing over to us, on behalf of certain underwriters, on part of the cargo per ship 'Turandot,' the proceeds of sale at Saigon of their interest, and we trust that your Lordship will consider that there has been such a denial of justice as your predecessor contemplated would warrant the interference of Her Majesty's Government on our behalf, and that your Lordship will be pleased now to direct Her Majesty's Ambassador at Berlin to interfere and procure us payment of the sum of 104,047*f.*, which was handed by the French to the German Government, for proceeds of sale at Saigon of the goods, for distribution to the parties entitled thereto.

We are, &c.,
(Signed)   SMITH, SUNDIUS, & Co.

(Translation.)   BERLIN: May 28, 1874.

In reply to your letter of the 15th instant, respecting the claim of the underwriters of various goods forming part of the cargo of the ship 'Turandot,' for payment of the proceeds of sale of the same, we have to inform you that the Imperial Chancellery, upon re-investigation of the circumstances, is not able to recognise the legal ground for said claim.

Signed for the Reichskanzlersamt,

Eck.

No. 9.

Mr. Lister to Messrs. Smith, Sundius, and Co.

FOREIGN OFFICE: September 24, 1874.

GENTLEMEN,—In reply to your letter of the 16th instant, respecting the case of the ship 'Turandot,' I am directed by the Earl of Derby to inform you that it is the opinion of Her Majesty's Government that the underwriters cannot claim to be in a better position than the owner of the ship, a German subject; and that as the German Government cannot be called upon under German law to repay the owner, Her Majesty's Government regret that they do not feel themselves in a position to support your claim.

I am, &c.,

(Signed) T. V. LISTER.

No. 10.

Messrs. Smith, Sundius, and Co. to the Earl of Derby.

(Received October 19.)

33 GRACECHURCH STREET, LONDON: October 19, 1874.

MY LORD,—We have to acknowledge receipt of your Lordship's communication dated the 24th of September, in which we are informed that in the opinion of Her Majesty's Government the underwriters whom we represent cannot claim to be in a better position than the owner of the ship, a German subject.

In reply we would first respectfully point out that the interest we represent is not, as your Lordship would appear to understand, in the ship, but in a portion of the cargo she had on board, as may be seen on reference to our letter to the Foreign Office dated the 1st of March, 1873.

We would next respectfully submit that your Lordship's hypothesis that the underwriters cannot claim to be in a better position than the owner of the ship (or goods), a German subject, accords entirely with the view the underwriters themselves take of their position, their opinion being that by reason of their having reimbursed the German shippers of the cargo the amount of loss under the policy of insurance, all interest in the subject-matter of the policy reverts to them, and that said interest is clearly defined by Article No. XIII. of the Treaty made at Frankfort on the 10th of May, 1871, which runs as follows:—

'Les bâtiments allemands qui étaient condamnés par les conseils de prises avant le 2 mars 1871 seront considérés comme condamnés définitivement. Ceux qui n'auraient pas été condamnés à la date susindiquée seront rendus avec la cargaison en tant qu'elle existe encore. Si la restitution des bâtiments et de la cargaison n'est plus possible, leur valeur, fixée d'après le prix de la rente, sera rendue à leurs propriétaires.'

Your Lordship will, we venture to hope, agree with us that the Article (No. XIII.) here cited is so clearly drawn up as to admit of but one construction, viz. that prizes, whether consisting of ships or cargoes, not condemned before the 2nd of March, 1871, shall be restored to their owners.

The following details of the capture and sale of the 'Turandot' and her cargo will, we would venture to hope, convince your Lordship of the entire justice of our demand, that the sale value of that portion of the 'Turandot's' cargo, the interest in which we, on behalf of our underwriters, represent, should be paid over to them by the German Government, to whom it was handed over by the French Government for that purpose, as can be shown by documents if needful:—

The German ship 'Turandot,' Captain Meinert, left Hamburg on the 10th April, 1870, bound for Hong Kong, having general cargo on board. On the 23rd of August,

1870, she was captured by the French war steamer 'Segond,' and was by her captors taken into Saigon, where she arrived on the 7th of September, and where she and her cargo were, without condemnation, sold, the proceeds of sale being remitted by the local authorities to the French Government at Versailles.

In accordance with Article No. XIII. of the Treaty of Peace before cited, the French Government dealt with the said proceeds (the vessel and cargo *never having been condemned*) in the manner described for such case by the Treaty; the proceeds of sale of cargo were—at least a letter from Versailles, dated the 3rd of August, 1872, signed by the Minister of Marine, informs us this was then being done—apportioned to the various shippers; the shippers belonging to neutral nationalities received the portions *direct* from the French Government, but the portions resulting from shipments made by *German* subjects were, for obvious reasons which your Lordship will readily appreciate, handed over by the French to the German Government for distribution to those entitled thereto.

Our letter to the Foreign Office dated the 1st of March, 1873, gives particulars of the goods shipped on board the 'Turandot' by Messrs. Schellhaas, Bade, and Co. to the consignment of Messrs. Edward Schellhaas and Co., of Hong Kong, which were insured by us for their value of 6,400*l.* This amount our underwriters paid to the assured, Messrs. Schellhaas, Bade, and Co., thereby acquiring a title to the goods, or to the proceeds of the sale thereof, amounting to 104,047*f.*, application for which sum has been made to, and rejected by, the Imperial Chancellery at Berlin, which continues to retain possession of it, thereby subjecting us to a denial of justice; and in laying the facts before your Lordship, more fully, perhaps, than heretofore, we respectfully crave your Lordship's earnest consideration of, and assistance in, the matter.

We are, &c.,

(Signed) SMITH, SUNDIUS, & CO.

No. 11.

Lord Tenterden to Messrs. Smith, Sundius, and Co.

FOREIGN OFFICE: October 26, 1874.

GENTLEMEN,—I am directed by the Earl of Derby to acknowledge the receipt of your letter of the 17th instant, containing further statements relative to the claim of the underwriters against the German Government for the insurance paid on account of the 'Turandot,' in consequence of her capture during the late Franco-German war, and I am, in reply, to inform you that your representations will receive the attention of Her Majesty's Government.

I am, &c.,

(Signed) TENTERDEN.

No. 12.

Lord Tenterden to Messrs. Smith, Sundius, and Co.

FOREIGN OFFICE : November 7, 1874.

GENTLEMEN,—The Earl of Derby referred to the Law Advisers of the Crown your further letter of the 17th ultimo, relative to the claim of the underwriters against the German Government, for the insurance paid on account of the German vessel 'Turandot,' in consequence of her capture during the late Franco-German war ; and I am now directed by his Lordship to inform you that he sees no reason to alter the opinion already expressed to you, that the decision of the German authorities in this matter cannot properly be questioned by Her Majesty's Government.

I am, &c.,

(Signed) TENTERDEN.

No. 13.

Messrs. Smith, Sundius, and Co. to the Earl of Derby.

(Received December 1.)

33 GRACECHURCH STREET, LONDON: November 26, 1874.

MY LORD,—We have to acknowledge receipt of your Lordship's communication, dated the 7th instant, informing us that having submitted this matter to the Law Advisers of the Crown, your Lordship sees no reason to alter the opinion that the decision of the German authorities cannot be questioned by Her Majesty's Government.

We have, in consequence, been led to review the relative positions of the German Government and the British underwriters in this matter, in order, if possible, to discover wherein lies the justice or legality of the retention by the German Government of money so manifestly belonging to British subjects, viz. 'of money arising from the sale of goods bought and paid for by the British underwriters,' whose right of property therein, or in the proceeds thereof, uninterruptedly continues, the said sale having been so completely acknowledged as wrongful that the proceeds thereof have been by them, as far as practicable, and in the words of the Treaty of Peace, 'rendus à leurs propriétaires,' or to the German Government as custodians for them. We are forced to confess that we fail to discover the justice or legality of said retention, and your Lordship's communication above referred to does not help us in this respect. We would therefore respectfully submit that the legal owners of the goods are alone entitled to the proceeds of their sale; that the underwriters, on paying to the shippers the value of the said goods under the policies, became, in accordance with the laws of all civilised nations, the legal owners thereof, that the capture and sale of the goods never having been confirmed by a 'Cour de Prises,' but on the contrary having been voided by the Treaty of Peace, the underwriters have never ceased to be the legal owners of the same; that the German Government, neither by virtue of the Treaty of Peace nor by International Law, or, we venture to assert, by their own laws, can claim any right of property in the proceeds arising from the sale of the goods; that the retention of such proceeds by said Government is therefore unjust and illegal; and that the underwriters, as sufferers of such illegality and injustice, are not unreasonable in still craving the assistance of Her Majesty's Government in the matter, and in cherishing the hope that the same help and protection which have lately been so actively extended in favour of a subject of Her Majesty by reason of alleged injustice suffered in a South American Republic, and in favour of another subject of Her Majesty by reason of injustice suffered in a Central American Republic, will not on reconsideration be denied to them, to obtain from a more potent power nearer home that justice their right to which obviously needs only to be amicably pointed out in order to be recognised and acknowledged.

We are, &c.,

(Signed) SMITH, SUNDIUS, & Co.

No. 14.

Lord Tenterden to Messrs. Smith, Sundius, and Co.

FOREIGN OFFICE: December 10, 1874.

GENTLEMEN,—I am directed by the Earl of Derby to acknowledge the receipt of your further letter of the 26th ultimo relative to the case of the 'Turandot,' and I am to state to you in reply that his Lordship sees no new facts in this representation to alter the opinion arrived at in regard to the case in question after consultation with the Law Officers.

I am, &c.,

(Signed) TENTERDEN.

(5.) CORRESPONDENCE RESPECTING THE CESSION OF FIJI, AND THE PROVISIONAL ARRANGEMENTS MADE FOR ADMINISTERING THE GOVERNMENT.

No. 1.

Governor Sir Hercules Robinson, K.C.M.G., to the Earl of Carnarvon.

(Received November 18.)

'PEARL,' ISLAND OF TAVIUNI, FIJI: October 3, 1874.

MY LORD,—As an opportunity occurs to-day for sending letters to England by the San Francisco mail steamer, I think it well, although the negotiations have not yet been finally concluded, to acquaint your Lordship with the progress that I have made so far in the mission with which I have been entrusted.

2. I left Sydney on the evening of the 12th ultimo, and after a passage of eleven days, including a detention of twenty-four hours at Norfolk Island, I arrived in Levuka harbour on the afternoon of the 23rd of September.

3. I at once learnt that the general feeling amongst the white settlers, and also amongst some of the natives, in favour of annexation was less strong than it had been in consequence of the recent debate in the House of Lords upon Fiji, a Report of which had been received at Levuka by the mail which had reached that port a few days before my arrival. Persons whose interests were adverse to the establishment of good government had taken advantage of expressions in your Lordship's speech as to the Crown right of pre-emption in all lands, and as regards the 'severe' form of government which would have to be adopted in the event of annexation, to excite distrust in the minds of both Europeans and natives on these subjects. The wildest reports were circulated. All private lands were to be confiscated, and Fiji was to be a penal settlement. Already 300 marines had left Portsmouth to

garrison the place and coerce the inhabitants! I merely mention these absurd rumours as their prevalence obliged me, in my subsequent negotiations, to correct as far as I could such mischievous misrepresentations.

4. Upon the day after my arrival, I paid a formal visit to Thakombau and four other principal ruling Chiefs, who had come to Levuka to meet me. I annex an extract from a local paper giving an account of this interview, during which no business was transacted; but I informed the King that whenever he felt inclined to enter upon business I would explain to him frankly and fully the object of my visit.

5. Upon the following day (25th of September) Thakombau came to see me by appointment on board Her Majesty's ship 'Dido' (the 'Pearl' being engaged in coaling), and we then discussed unreservedly the question of annexation in all its bearings. I placed clearly before the King the views of Her Majesty's Government. At first Thakombau seemed much depressed and reserved, but before the close of the interview, which lasted for more than two hours, he became cheerful and communicative, illustrating the opinions which he expressed with much force and humour, and in a manner which showed clearly that he perfectly apprehended the points under discussion, At the commencement of the interview he said he would take time to think of his position, and would consult with the other Chiefs as to what was best to be done; but towards the close he expressed himself strongly in favour of an unconditional cession of the Islands to the Queen, observing that 'any Fijian Chief who refuses to cede cannot have much wisdom. . . . If matters remain as they are, Fiji will become like a piece of drift-wood on the sea, and be picked up by the first passer-by. . . . By annexation the two races, white and black, will be bound together, and it will be impossible to sever them. The "interlacing" has come. Fijians as a nation are of an unstable character, and a white man who wishes to get anything out of a Fijian, if he does not succeed in his object to-day, will try again to-morrow, until the Fijian is either wearied out or over-persuaded, and gives in. But law will bind

us together, and the stronger nation will lend stability to the weaker.'

6. The result of the interview was, I think, on the whole entirely satisfactory, and the views expressed by the King displayed so much intelligence and unselfishness that I am sure your Lordship will feel interested in perusing a full report of the conversation. I accordingly enclose a copy of the notes which were taken down at the time by a member of my personal staff, who was present during the interview.

7. Upon the 28th it was intimated to me by a message from the King that, after two days' discussion in Council, he and the other Chiefs then present in Levuka had agreed to the following resolution :—

'We give Fiji unreservedly to the Queen of Britain, that she may rule us justly and affectionately, and that we may live in peace and prosperity.'

8. I then forwarded to the King a draft of a Deed of Cession which I had prepared, and stated that, when it had been interpreted and fully explained to the Chiefs, I would be prepared to accept the signatures of such of them as were in Levuka, and on its execution by the remainder of the ruling authorities I would formally accept the cession, and establish a provisional Government until Her Majesty's pleasure as to the future constitution of the islands could be known.

9. The following day (the 29th) was devoted by the Chiefs to the consideration of the Deed of Cession, and in the evening it was intimated to me that the King and Chiefs would be prepared to sign at Nasova, the public offices of Levuka, on the morning of the 30th of September.

10. I accordingly proceeded to Nasova at ten o'clock on the morning of the 30th, when the King read and handed to me the formal resolution of the Council giving Fiji unreservedly to the Queen. The Deed of Cession was then read in Fijian, and the instrument executed by the King and the four other ruling Chiefs who were present. I enclose a minute of the proceedings, with copies attached of the resolution of Council and Deed of Cession.

11. I then invited Thakombau to accompany me on a tour of the islands to obtain the signatures of Maafu and of the other Chiefs not then in Levuka, whose assent was necessary to the validity of the cession. This he at once cheerfully agreed to, and we left Levuka the same afternoon in Her Majesty's ships 'Pearl' and 'Dido' for Loma-Loma, Maafu's capital, at which place we arrived on the morning of the 1st instant.

12. That day was occupied in receiving and paying visits of ceremony; and on the morning of the 2nd Thakombau brought Maafu, the Chief of Lau, and Tui Thakau, the Chief of Thakaundrové, on board the 'Pearl,' when the Deed of Cession was fully explained to and executed by them. I enclose a copy of the notes of the meeting.

13. I am now on my way to Ritova, the Chief of Mathuata in Vanua Levu, and propose, when I have received his assent to the cession, to return to Levuka, where I hope to find assembled the few remaining Chiefs whose signatures it is desirable to obtain.

Practically, however, with Thakombau's, Maafu's, and Tui Thakau's unconditional tender of cession, the question may be considered as disposed of.

14. When the Chiefs have all executed the deed, I shall formally accept the country in the Queen's name, and assume the administration of the Government.

15. There is one clause in the Deed of Cession upon which I think it as well to make here a few explanatory observations. I refer to clause 4, which deals with the land, a question which has given me much anxious consideration. If I had avoided all specific reference to land in the deed, restricting it to a simple unconditional cession of the Sovereignty of Fiji, such a course would, I feel sure, have given rise to future difficulties and complications, and, probably, charges of breach of faith. Considering that all writers upon the land question, from Consul Prichard down to the present time, have agreed that every acre of land in Fiji is private property, it would unquestionably have been contended that a mere cession of sovereignty did not convey the absolute proprietorship of the soil. If, on the other hand, any clause had been inserted transfer-

ring to Her Majesty the possession of all lands irrespective of private ownership, and the requirements of various tribes, such a provision would never have been assented to peacefully, and the attempt to insert it would, I think, have fairly lent a colour to the rumours of confiscation and spoliation of private rights which had been so industriously circulated. I accordingly determined, after lengthened conferences with Mr. Innes, the Attorney-General of New South Wales, by whom I am accompanied as legal adviser, to insert the clause 4 in the shape in which it will be found in the accompanying copy of the Instrument of Cession. The clause simply vests in Her Majesty the absolute ownership of all lands not shown by those laying claim to them to be *bonâ fide* the property of Europeans or other foreigners, or not required for the maintenance and support of Chiefs and tribes, leaving Her Majesty's Government to be the ultimate judge as to what lands have been fairly acquired by Europeans, and what extent is required for the support of the natives. It would have been impossible to have gone further than this without injustice, and without giving rise at the outset of British rule to serious disaffection and difficulties. The clause as it stands is in unison with native feeling and precedent, and is, I think, satisfactory to all except such of the whites as entertain doubts regarding the *bonâ fide* character of their titles. As showing how thoroughly the proposal is understood by the native mind, I enclose a copy of a question put in Council by Ratu Savanaca when the Chiefs were discussing clause 4 of the Deed of Cession; he expressed satisfaction at the proposed settlement, but asked how about the disposal of land assigned to the Government for the use of Chiefs and tribes. Would the parties to whom such lands might be allotted have the right to sell or assign, or would the Crown claim the right of pre-emption? In reply to this enquiry, which was brought to me informally through Mr. Wilkinson the interpreter, I intimated that the consideration of these points would form an important element in the labours of the Commission to be appointed for the purpose of enquiring into and determining upon the whole land question, and that these and other points would be settled in the manner which should be shown to be most just and advantageous for the interests of the Chiefs and Tribes. It will be a matter for serious consideration whether, having regard to the improvident character of the natives, it will be good policy to confer upon them the right of absolutely disposing of their property.

16. I shall not fail to advise your Lordship fully by the next opportunity of the further progress of negotiations; but I cannot delay this letter longer, as I am obliged to despatch it by special boat for Levuka this morning to catch the mail steamer for San Francisco, which is expected to-morrow.

I have, &c.,
(Signed) HERCULES ROBINSON.

No. 2.

The Earl of Carnarvon to Sir Hercules Robinson, K.C.M.G.

DOWNING STREET: December 10, 1874.

SIR,—I have the honour to acknowledge the receipt of your Report of the 3rd of October, containing an account of the progress of negotiations since your arrival at Levuka, and transmitting, with other documents, a copy of the Instrument of Cession by which the Fiji Islands were formally given over to Her Majesty.

2. I have laid your despatch before the Queen, who has read it with interest, and Her Majesty commands me to convey to you her approval of the ability, discretion, and energy with which you have conducted this transaction to a successful and satisfactory issue.

3. Writing, as I do at present, without full information as to the details of your arrangements for the temporary administration of the Government, I can, of course, only express in general terms my opinion of their apparent adequacy to meet the requirements of the case; but I feel so much confidence in your judgment, that I am satis-

fied that the dispositions which you have made will, when explained and laid before me in full, be found calculated to enable the more permanent administration of the Government to be entered upon with the least possible difficulty, and with all reasonable promise of success.

4. I have already expressed my thanks to your Ministers for their ready and valuable co-operation in this important matter, but I must also request you to convey to Mr. Innes, the Attorney-General of New South Wales, who accompanied you in the capacity of legal adviser, my appreciation of the able assistance which he rendered to you.

I have, &c.,

(Signed) CARNARVON.

No. 3.

Sir Hercules Robinson, K.C.M.G., to the Earl of Carnarvon.

(Received December 19.)

'PEARL,' LEVUKA, FIJI: October 11, 1874.

MY LORD,—In continuation of my despatch sent on the 3rd instant from the Island of Taviuni, I have now the honour to report that I went from thence along the north coast of Vanua Levu, touching at Nanduri and Mathuata. Here we found that a tribal war had a few days before broken out between the rival Chiefs Ritova and Katonivere, which had resulted in loss of life and considerable destruction of property. Our arrival at the moment with Thakombau and two ships of war was opportune. Thakombau at once sent for all the parties concerned; explained to them what had taken place in Levuka and Loma-Loma, and that he was going round the group to make arrangements for the transfer of the government of the country to the Queen. He ordered both contending parties to disperse forthwith to their homes, and to take down the war fences. He also carried away with him, in the 'Dido,' the two Chiefs Ritova and

Katonivere, with a view of investigating their conduct in Levuka, with the assistance of the other ruling Chiefs.

2. Peace having thus been restored on the Mathuata coast, we proceeded round the north-west point of Vanua Levu to Bua, where we landed, inspected a portion of this well-governed native province, and took away with us the Chief Tui Bua, to be present at the proposed gathering of all the Chiefs in Levuka, with a view to the formal transfer of the country to the British Crown.

3. On the 7th of October I returned to Levuka, and on the 10th I proceeded by appointment to the Government Buildings at Nasova, where all the Chiefs who had not previously signed the Deed of Cession attached their names and seals to the instrument, which was then executed by me, and a counterpart handed to Thakombau, to be retained by himself and the other high Chiefs as a record of the transaction.

4. I then publicly declared Fiji to be from that time forth a Possession and Dependency of the British Crown, and hoisted the British flag with the usual formalities. I enclose a minute of the proceedings, in which will be found a description of an interesting incident which occurred when Thakombau presented to me his favourite war club, for transmission to Her Majesty.

5. Upon the afternoon of the same day I issued the first 'Government Gazette' of the Colony of Fiji, copies of which are herewith enclosed. It contains a Proclamation declaring Fiji to be a British Dependency, and announcing that I had assumed the temporary administration of the Government of the Islands until Her Majesty's pleasure could be made known as to the constitution of the permanent Government of the Colony. I published in the same Gazette, for general information, in both English and Fijian, copies of the Resolution adopted by the Chiefs assembled in Council, giving Fiji unreservedly to the Queen, and of the Deed of Cession which had that day been executed at Nasova.

6. In a subsequent despatch I will report to your Lordship the arrangements which I may make for the establishment of a provisional Administration, pending

the notification of Her Majesty's pleasure as regards the permanent Government of these Islands.

I have, &c.,

(Signed) HERCULES ROBINSON.

No. 4.
Sir Hercules Robinson, K.C.M.G., to the Earl of Carnarvon.
(Received December 19.)

'PEARL,' FIJI: October 11, 1874.

MY LORD,—I have the honour to report that, after the formal execution yesterday by all the Chiefs of the Deed of Cession, Thakombau stated that he desired to say a few words to me, and asked that Mr. Thurston, to whom he had that morning explained his wishes, might be allowed to interpret them. Mr. Thurston then said:—

'Your Excellency, before finally ceding his country to Her Majesty the Queen of Great Britain and Ireland, the King desires, through your Excellency, to give to Her Majesty the only thing he possesses that may interest her.

'The King gives Her Majesty his old and favourite war club, the former and, until lately, the only known law of Fiji.

'In abandoning club law, and adopting the forms and principles of civilised societies, he laid by his old weapon, and covered it with the emblems of peace. Many of his people, whole tribes, died and passed away under the old law, but hundreds of thousands still survive to learn and enjoy the newer and better state of things. The King adds only a few words. With this emblem of the past he sends his love to Her Majesty, saying that he fully confides in her and her children, who, succeeding her, shall become Kings of Fiji, to exercise a watchful control over the welfare of his children and people, who, having survived the barbaric law and age, are now submitting themselves, under Her Majesty's rule, to civilisation.'

Thakombau then handed the club to me; and I informed him that I would not fail to transmit it to the Queen, and would at the same time convey to Her Majesty, through your Lordship, the message which he desired should accompany the gift.

I will forward the box containing the club by the first convenient opportunity.

I have, &c.,

(Signed)   HERCULES ROBINSON.

No. 5.

Sir Hercules Robinson, K.C.M.G., to the Earl of Carnarvon.

(Received December 19.)

'PEARL,' LEVUKA, FIJI: October 16, 1874.

MY LORD,—The formalities for the transfer of the sovereignty of these islands to Her Majesty having been completed on the 10th instant, I proceeded at once, as authorised by your Lordship, to authorise a temporary Administration, pending provision being made by Letters Patent or Order in Council for the permanent government of the Colony. The accompanying 'Fiji Gazettes,' numbered 1 to 6 consecutively, will show fully in detail the various measures adopted by me for this purpose.

2. The question as to how provision could best be made for supervising the temporary administration of the government gave me much consideration. There was no person in Fiji who had had any experience of a Crown Colony. It was clear to me, too, that much would depend upon the manner in which affairs were conducted upon the first establishment of British rule, and that it would have been scarcely practicable for your Lordship's Department to have exercised any effectual control over the Provisional Government if I had placed it in direct communication with Downing Street. I therefore determined, as Sydney is now connected by means of regular monthly steamers with Levuka, and is at the same time in telegraphic communication with London, to retain in my own

hands, for the present, a general supervision over the temporary administration of the newly-established Colony.

3. As I had no information whatever respecting the intentions of Her Majesty's Government with regard to the future disposal of the services of Mr. Layard, the Consul for Fiji and Tonga, I requested him to continue to act as Consul for Tonga, and at the same time to accept the unpaid offices of Vice-President of the Executive Council and Administrator of the Government in my absence, drawing, as heretofore, his emoluments from the Foreign Office until your Lordship had had an opportunity of determining upon the permanent establishments for Fiji, and the Foreign Office should decide as to the Tongan Consulship. This Mr. Layard at once acceded to, so that, for the present, as will be seen on a reference to the accompanying papers, the revenues of the Colony are not subjected to any charge for either the Governor or the Administrator of the Government.

4. In like manner I requested Mr. Innes, the Attorney-General of New South Wales, by whom I am accompanied, to accept a seat in the Executive Council without office, both for the benefit of the assistance which he could render me while here, and also to enable me, on my return to New South Wales, to obtain the advantage of his legal knowledge and sound judgment in all Fiji matters which may be transmitted for my decision.

5. I completed the Executive Council by the appointments, as will be seen from Gazette No. 1, of Mr. Thurston as Colonial Secretary, Mr. Horton as Treasurer, and Mr. Swanston as Secretary for Native Affairs, assigning to each a salary for the present of 400*l*. a year. These appointments appear to give general satisfaction. Mr. Thurston is certainly the fittest person in Fiji to act as Colonial Secretary. He is intimately acquainted with the circumstances and requirements of the group; he is a good Fijian scholar, and he served as Acting Consul here for some years to the entire satisfaction, I understand, of the Foreign Office. Mr. Horton is the Manager of the Fijian Banking Company, and a gentleman upon whose integrity the utmost reliance may be placed. The arrange-

ment, too, will effect a considerable saving, as the receipts and disbursements of the Government will be made through the Bank, thus rendering unnecessary the services of more than one subordinate Treasury Officer, an Accountant. Mr. Swanston held the office of Minister for Native Affairs under the Constitutional Government of Fiji, and has the reputation of being an honest, independent man, sincerely desirous of advancing the interests of the native population of the country. Amongst these three officers I have distributed the supervision of all the administrative and judicial departments of the Government, dividing the functions in the manner which will be found specified in a notification published in the Gazette of the 13th instant (No. 2).

6. In the Judicial Department I have been enabled to make considerable reductions. The office of Chief Justice and Chancellor of the Kingdom has been allowed to lapse; and I have appointed one officer to discharge the duties of Judge of the Central Court of Fiji and Chief Magistrate of the Colony. All the offices established under this head will be found specified in the Gazette of the 14th instant (No. 5); and I need merely remark here that the saving on the Judicial Department amounts to over 800*l.* a year, as compared with the expenditure under that head during the *ad interim* arrangement which I found in existence on my arrival.

7. The native armed constabulary appeared to me to stand in need of immediate reorganisation. Grave statements have been publicly urged against the men of this force, charging them with outrages and cruelties perpetrated upon the helpless population of the country districts, especially upon women; and I fear that too many of these charges were well founded. It was clear to me that the force should at once be considerably reduced in numbers, and placed under strict supervision and control. I accordingly determined to reduce the strength to 200 picked men—a number amply sufficient to maintain order throughout the whole group—and to place the force under the superintendence of Lieutenant Olive, of the Royal Marines, whose services were kindly placed at my dis-

posal by Commodore Goodenough for this purpose. I enclose a copy of the correspondence which I have had with Commodore Goodenough on this subject. I may add that Lieutenant Olive appears to me to combine firmness of character with gentleness of disposition to an extent which has already endeared him to the natives, and which renders him peculiarly fitted for the delicate and responsible position in which he is placed. The total cost of police, including rations, clothing, &c., will amount to but little more than 3,000*l.* a year.

8. The appointments necessary for the efficient administration of native affairs received my careful consideration. Eventually I determined, with the advice of the Executive Council, upon the following departmental arrangements :—Four European Stipendiary Magistrates have been created for the trial of European and mixed cases throughout the whole group. The districts and places at which Courts are to be held will be found specified in Schedule A, attached to Gazette No. 6, of the 15th instant. The islands were next divided into twelve provinces, over each of which a Provincial Chief styled Roko and a native Stipendiary Magistrate were appointed. These provinces were next subdivided into eighty-two districts in charge of Bulis, each Buli being placed in the first, second, or third class, according to the number of villages under his control. By this machinery it is believed that arrangements can be made for the efficient government of the natives, under the general supervision of the Secretary for Native Affairs, without departing in any important particular from their own official customs, traditions, and boundaries. The total cost of the Department, including the salary of the Protector of Imported Polynesian Labourers, amounts to a little more than 5,800*l.* a year. I enclose a map showing the boundaries of the twelve provinces, and Schedules B, C, and D, in the Appendix to the Estimates, will furnish the names of the twelve Rokos, the twelve Native Stipendiary Magistrates, and the eighty-two Bulis, with the name of the province or district in charge of each.

9. The remaining subordinate provisional appoint-

ments, which will all be found detailed in Gazette No. 5, do not appear to me to call for any remark. The salaries have in each case been fixed at the lowest practicable amount consistent with the efficiency of the public service. The total cost of all the establishments of the Colony amounts, as will be seen by the return published in Gazette No. 6, to 13,568*l.* per annum, and the services, exclusive of establishments, to 4,334*l.*, making the total authorised expenditure for Fiji, for the year ending 10th October, 1875, at the rate of 17,902*l.* per annum.

10. Gazette No. 2 contains the Customs tariff and other dues and taxes, which, with the advice of the Executive Council, I authorised the Provisional Government to collect. The former tariff was composed almost entirely of *ad valorem* duties, which here, as elsewhere, have been found to be unequal as well as demoralising in their application. The total receipts of the Customs duties of Fiji for the year ended the 30th of September, 1874, amounted to 10,254*l.* I determined to substitute for this tariff the tariff lately adopted in New South Wales, and which is composed entirely of specific duties on about forty-five articles of general consumption. It is estimated that this tariff will produce in Fiji a revenue of about 15,000*l.* a year. The tonnage dues have been abolished, and pilotage rates, light dues, and annual licenses continued at the same rate as heretofore, the only increase being a license fee of 10*l.*, instead of 2*l.* 10*s.*, upon Polynesian immigrant vessels for each voyage, it being thought fair to make these vessels contribute to a larger extent than formerly to the expense of the supervision which it is necessary to exercise over the foreign labour traffic.

11. An entire change has been made in the system of native taxation. Heretofore the amount of the tax was uniform throughout the group, being 20*s.* for each man and 4*s.* for each woman. There being little ready money amongst the natives, payment has been accepted in kind, and the tax collector has been accompanied by a broker whose custom it was to take over at a low valuation the agricultural produce, fishing-nets, sleeping-mats, axes, &c., and other articles of domestic use and convenience which

the people had to part with and sacrifice to meet the demands of the Government. In some districts the people were too poor to be able to satisfy the tax even in this manner; and painful accounts have recently been published in the newspapers as to the wholesale way in which the entire male population of large districts have been removed from their homes, and their services in effect sold to such of the European planters as were willing to pay to the Government the tax, with the costs that had accrued in instituting legal proceedings for its recovery. I enclose some letters extracted from the local press upon this subject, and to which my attention was directed soon after my arrival. I particularly would invite your Lordship's perusal of a letter published in the 'Fiji Times' of the 7th of October, under the signature of Dr. Langham, the head of the Wesleyan Mission in Fiji. Dr. Langham called upon me and narrated to me atrocities and cruelties in connection with the Government system of raising the native taxes for the truth of which he stated that he was prepared to vouch. These representations convinced me of the necessity of making a change in the amount of the native tax and the mode of enforcing it. I accordingly determined that women should be exempt; that the tax in kind should not be enforced; that every male Fijian between the ages of sixteen and sixty should contribute twenty days' labour upon the public works of his province, being allowed to commute his service for $6d.$, $4\frac{1}{2}d.$, or $3d.$ a day—i.e. $10s.$, $7s.$ $6d.$, or $5s.$—according to the local circumstances of the district wherein he may reside. A capitation tax of $10s.$ on each imported Polynesian labourer is also imposed, such tax to be paid quarterly by the employers.

12. I directed further that all native taxes in arrear at the date of cession should be remitted, and that all Fijians who as defaulting taxpayers had been removed from their homes and placed in service with European settlers should forthwith be liberated, the planters being compensated for any sum paid on account of the tax due by each labourer less the value of the time actually served. The notifications embodying all these regulations as

regards native taxes will be found at p. 9 of Gazette No. 2.

13. Gazette No. 6 publishes for general information a Return showing the estimated revenue and authorised expenditure of the Colony for the year ending the 10th of October, 1875. The revenue is estimated at 23,875*l.*, and the authorised expenditure amounts to 17,902*l.*, showing an excess of estimated revenue over authorised expenditure of 5,973*l*. I should mention, however, that the expenditure only provides for the payment of Thakombau's allowance at the reduced rate of 900*l.*, which he received during the *ad interim* Consular Government, and it makes no provision for a salary for the Governor, upon both of which points I propose to address your Lordship in a subsequent despatch.

14. Gazette No. 3 contains a Proclamation making provision for the administration of criminal and civil justice in Fiji, pending the signification of Her Majesty's pleasure as regards the permanent laws of the Colony.

15. Gazette No. 4 provides for the regulation and control of the hiring and service of Polynesian immigrants, and the carrying of such immigrants on board vessels. It also notifies the appointment of twenty gentlemen to be Justices of the Peace for the Colony of Fiji.

16. With a view to avoid further complications of the land question by persons speculating in doubtful titles of both Europeans and natives, I caused a notification to be inserted in the Gazette intimating that no sale, transfer, or assignment of land, or of any interest therein made subsequent to the date of cession, will be recognised by the Government pending the settlement of existing titles to land. This notification will be found at p. 9 of Gazette No. 2.

17. Having thus completed all the arrangements necessary for the establishment of a Provisional Government, I propose leaving Fiji this afternoon for Sydney, and hope to arrive there nearly a week in advance of the date originally contemplated for my return.

I have, &c.,
(Signed)   HERCULES ROBINSON.

No. 6.

Sir Hercules Robinson, K.C.M.G., to the Earl of Carnarvon.

(Received December 19.)

'PEARL,' at sea en route to SYDNEY: October 17, 1874.

MY LORD,—Before leaving Levuka I paid a farewell visit to Thakombau and the other principal Chiefs who had assembled there from different parts of the group to confer with me upon the business of my mission.

2. As it may interest your Lordship to peruse the observations made by Thakombau and Maafu at this interview, I enclose notes of the conversation which took place on the occasion.

I have, &c.,

(Signed) HERCULES ROBINSON.

Enclosure in No. 6.

Notes of a Meeting between his Excellency Sir Hercules Robinson and the Vunivalu and Chiefs at Dryimba, on Thursday, October 15, 1874.

At 3 P.M. his Excellency Sir Hercules Robinson, accompanied by Commodore Goodenough and the Honourable J. G. L. Innes, and by Mr. Wilkinson, the Chief Interpreter of the Government, proceeded by appointment to pay a farewell visit to Thakombau and the other Chiefs. Sir Hercules Robinson was received by the Vunivalu, Maafu, and all the other Chiefs who signed the cession, except Ratu Epeli, who had been obliged to leave for Bau, and Ratu Isikeli, who was also absent on duty.

Upon being seated, Sir Hercules Robinson said—

'Vunivalu and Chiefs, as I leave to-morrow morning for Sydney, I have come here to-day to bid you all farewell. I have been greatly pleased with my visit to this country. I have been much struck by the beauty and fertility of the islands, and I trust I may have an opportunity of revisiting you on some future occasion. When you return to your respective Provinces, I hope you will explain fully to those under you what has taken place between us in Levuka, and that you will both by precept and example impress upon your people the advantages of industry and good order.

'Having had experience of native races elsewhere, I know that with them hasty changes are difficult and undesirable. The people must be led forward step by step; and, in framing a new system for the government of this country under the Queen, I have accordingly tried to carry out, as far as possible, what I understand to be your wishes, and to adhere at present as closely as practicable to native official customs, boundaries, and traditions.

'My object is, that the Provisional British Government which I have established should gain the respect, the confidence, and the affection of both Chiefs and people; and I trust you will all co-operate with me in giving effect to this policy.

'Although I am leaving Fiji I shall continue, until Her Majesty can make some permanent appointment, to watch over the interests of the country. If any Chief or other Fijian should feel that he is aggrieved, he will only have to communicate with me by a petition to insure for his complaint prompt attention and investigation.

'I will only, in conclusion, say one word as to the past and the future. As regards the past, I hope that all differences and animosities will now be forgotten and subdued. The Vunivalu's ['Root of War'] war club has been sent with a dutiful and loving message to our Queen. I hope all other weapons of strife have in like manner been buried at the foot of the staff upon which we have raised the Union Jack.

'As regards the future, it is in your hands. As the Vunivalu said to me the other day, "the future of Fiji is Britain." And you must all remember that whilst British rule is mild it is at the same time firm and all-powerful. You are now servants of the Queen, and if you cannot each of you in your respective provinces govern the people in accordance with what Her Majesty's Government may think just and right, you will have to give place to those who can more correctly appreciate the obligations of the position. I trust no such necessity may arise, but in these matters it is true kindness to be frank and explicit.

'I have finished. But one word more. Believe me that, in accepting the trouble and responsibility of the government of Fiji, the Queen has but one desire—the good government of the country and the contentment and happiness of all classes of the population.'

After a pause, during which Thakombau signed to Maafu to speak first, but the latter would not do so, Thakombau spoke as follows:—

'I am glad to hear what the Governor has said on his coming to say good-bye, and I am pleased to be able to say that from the Governor's first arrival up to the present time we have understood all that he has said and desired. I am glad on this occasion to hear such words of counsel, consideration, and goodness; and I hope that all present will now understand that they are Her Majesty's subjects and servants, and that, as the Governor has said, their future is in their own hands. They will be judged according to their behaviour and their deserts, and according to such judgment they will stand or fall.

'We know that we are not here now simply as an independent body of Fijian Chiefs, but as subordinate agents of the British Crown, and being bound together by strength and power, that strength and power will be able to overcome anything which tends to interfere with or interrupt the present unity.

'Any Chief attempting to pursue a course of disloyalty must expect to be dealt with on his own merits, and not to escape by any subterfuge, or by relying upon any Fijian customs or upon his high family connexions.'

Maafu then said—

'What more can any of us say? The unity of to-day has been our desire for years. I have now been twenty years in Fiji, and I have never before seen such a sight as I see to-day—Fiji actually and truly united. We tried a Government ourselves; we did not succeed. That has passed away. Another, and a better and more permanent, state of things has been brought into existence. I believe that I speak the mind of all present when I say that we are really and truly united in heart and will, and we are all gratified with what we have heard. We are true men, and will return to our homes knowing that the unity of Fiji is a fact, and that peace and prosperity will follow.'

The meeting shortly afterwards closed; and Sir Hercules Robinson, accompanied by Commodore Goodenough, the Hon. J. G. L. Innes, and Mr. Wilkinson, returned on board Her Majesty's ship 'Pearl.'

(Signed)   J. GEO. LONG INNES.

No. 7.

Sir Hercules Robinson, K.C.M.G., to the Earl of Carnarvon.

(Received December 19.)

'PEARL,' at sea en route to SYDNEY: October 18, 1874.

MY LORD,—I have the honour to forward, for your Lordship's information, a copy of an address which was presented to me before leaving Levuka, on behalf of the Wesleyan Missionaries stationed in Fiji, together with a copy of my reply.

I have, &c.,

(Signed)   HERCULES ROBINSON.

Enclosure 1 in No. 7.

To his Excellency Sir Hercules George Robert Robinson, Knight Commander of the Most Distinguished Order of St. Michael and St. George, Governor, Commander-in-Chief, and Vice-Admiral of the Colony of New South Wales and its Dependencies, Governor of Norfolk Island, and provisionally Governor of Fiji.

May it please your Excellency—

On behalf of the Wesleyan Ministers now resident in the Colony of Fiji, we beg to assure your Excellency of

I

our intense satisfaction with the cession of the Islands of Fiji to Her Majesty the Queen of Great Britain and Ireland.

As the Church to which we belong has ever proved itself most loyal to the British Crown, we feel we only act as spokesmen for our absent brethren the Wesleyan Ministers of Fiji, if we beg of your Excellency to receive our assurance of continued loyalty to Her Majesty the Queen.

Your Excellency will allow us to say that, in our opinion, our work as Christian missionaries would have received serious injury but for the proclamation of British sovereignty.

We trust that your Excellency's administration of the government will be the means of preventing evils in connection with a form of slavery, of the existence of which your Excellency is doubtless aware.

We desire to express our gratitude to Her Majesty's Government for your Excellency's appointment as Special Commissioner; we also wish to convey to your Excellency our appreciation of the services rendered to the cause of civilisation by Commodore Goodenough and Mr. Consul Layard.

We venture to remind your Excellency that it is not forty years since missionaries representing the British Wesleyan Churches came to Fiji, then in a state of savage heathenism, and that, but for the blessing of God upon their labours, there would have been no British Fiji at the present day.

We pray God's continued blessing on your Excellency's administration of the government of Fiji, and trust that your Excellency will ever be under Divine guidance.

Wishing your Excellency a safe voyage,

    (Signed) JOSEPH WATERHOUSE,
           SAMUEL W. BROOKS,
           D. S. WYLIE.

Enclosure 2 in No. 7.

NASOVA: October 14, 1874.

REVEREND GENTLEMEN,—I thank you sincerely for the loyal and cordial Address which you have presented to me, and for the congratulations which you have been so good as to offer me upon the annexation of Fiji to the British Crown.

I entirely concur with you in the appreciation which you are so good as to express of the services rendered to Fiji by Commodore Goodenough and Mr. Consul Layard. The success which has attended my Mission is largely attributable to the care and ability with which those gentlemen had previously investigated the circumstances and requirements of the country.

I fervently trust that a new era has now dawned upon Fiji, and that under British rule the moral as well as the material progress of the New Colony may, by the blessing of Providence, be effectually secured. The great social advances which have already been made within the last forty years from savage heathenism are due to the self-denying and unostentatious labours of the Wesleyan Church; and I can therefore heartily wish to your missionary enterprise in this country continued vitality and success.

With renewed thanks for the good wishes which you are pleased to express for myself personally, I have, &c.,

(Signed) HERCULES ROBINSON.

To the Rev. Joseph Waterhouse,
,, Samuel Brooks,
,, D. S. Wylie.

No. 8.

Sir Hercules Robinson, K.C.M.G., to the Earl of Carnarvon.

(Received December 19.)

PEARL,' at sea en route to SYDNEY: October 18, 1874.

MY LORD,—I enclose for your Lordship's information a copy of the letter of instructions which I addressed to

Mr. Layard before leaving Fiji, pointing out to him the course which I thought it desirable for him to pursue while acting as my deputy in the temporary administration of the Provisional Government.

I have, &c.,

(Signed)   HERCULES ROBINSON.

No. 9.
The Earl of Carnarvon to Sir Hercules Robinson, G.C.M.G.

DOWNING STREET: January 16, 1875.

SIR,—I have deferred any general reply to your despatches (which have been duly acknowledged in the usual manner) giving an account of your proceedings in Fiji, and the steps taken by you for receiving the cession of the islands, and establishing in them a provisional Government, until I should have been made fully acquainted, as I am by your later communications, with all details. Those which have now been received by the last mail appear to me to complete, as far as possible, the history of past transactions, and of the arrangements which you think may suffice until a duly constituted Colonial Government can be established.

2. I have already conveyed to you the Queen's gracious approval of the manner in which you have executed the responsible mission for which you were selected, and I have notified to you by telegraph that Her Majesty has been pleased to mark her sense of the service thus rendered by you by promoting you to the Grand Cross of the Order of St. Michael and St. George.

3. I at the same time acquainted you that Her Majesty had been pleased to recognise the special services of Mr. Innes, the Attorney-General of New South Wales, who accompanied you to Fiji, by conferring upon him a knighthood.

4. I have on a previous occasion expressed my sense of the readiness with which your Ministers have on all occasions endeavoured to assist you in carrying out your

instructions; and it would not be right for me to omit to refer to the valuable services rendered by Mr. Consul Layard and Commodore Goodenough during the difficult period which intervened between the presentation of their Report and the cession of Fiji.

5. Your account of your transactions with Thakombau and the other chiefs is very clear and satisfactory, and I fully approve of the explanations afforded by you as to the terms on which only Her Majesty's Government could consent to accept the cession. The Articles, also, of the Instrument of Cession appear fully to meet the requirements of the case.

6. The provision which you made for the temporary administration of the Government was doubtless as complete as circumstances permitted, and I trust that the provisional establishment may prove adequate to the requirements of the period which must elapse before a more efficient Government can be constituted, but which I am endeavouring to make as short as possible.

7. I have pleasure in acquainting you that the Queen has been pleased to appoint the Honourable Sir Arthur H. Gordon, K.C.M.G., to be the first Governor of Fiji. Sir Arthur Gordon's ability, and his administrative experience in Colonies in which the coloured inhabitants form a large majority of the population, will, I doubt not, qualify him in a special degree for the work of organising the new Government. He will probably sail for Fiji early in March next.

8. It is perhaps possible that on the expiration of his term of government the administration of affairs in Fiji will be found to be so well established as to permit of the Colony being entrusted to a Governor of less high standing, and that some economy in the salary of the Governor may consequently be effected; but I am satisfied that there could be no greater mistake than to commit to weak or inexperienced hands the solution of such difficult questions as those which will have to be met at the outset in taking over the new dependency of Fiji.

9. For the same reason, while I am obliged to you for the careful estimate which you have made of the probable

revenue of the Colony, and for your calculations of the administrative staff which may be provided without exceeding that estimate, I do not think that, when once the present provisional Administration is replaced by a permanent one, the salaries which you have mentioned would suffice to secure the services of competent Civil Officers. I am most desirous to ensure all practicable economy, but when I reflect that every Department has to be created and organised on proper principles, and that, in the first instance, if possible, more than ever high character and ability are indispensable in those who are to hold the principal appointments, I cannot but feel that there would be little hope of procuring really effective service from persons receiving much smaller remunerations than are given in similar cases in Australia or other Colonies.

10. I apprehend, therefore, that some increase upon your estimate of the cost of the Civil Establishment is inevitable; and, indeed, I assume that your calculations have been in a great degree governed by the opinion that the administration of affairs in Fiji might be placed under the surveillance of the Governor of New South Wales, and would in that case be less dependent upon the efficiency of the local staff—a course which, as you are now aware, is not contemplated by Her Majesty's Government.

11. I have, in conclusion, to thank you for your careful examination of the difficult questions connected with the liabilities of Fiji, the titles to land, and other special points which have to be dealt with. These subjects are receiving my careful consideration, and I shall in due course give such instructions to Sir A. Gordon as may be requisite.

I have, &c.,

(Signed)   CARNARVON.

CHAPTER III.

PRÉCIS OF A MORE ADVANCED CHARACTER.

THE student has now been exercised in giving succinct accounts of the contents of various documents in series. It has been necessary for him, especially in the longer correspondence, to read through and bear in mind the relations of one letter to another, and to acquire an intelligent view of a long and sometimes complicated case. But his mental work has been principally to sift the correspondence for its facts, and produce them in the order in which they were written. But before he can claim to understand précis-writing in its higher branches he must be able not only to do this, but, in addition to taking to pieces and reconstructing on a smaller scale, he must learn to compare different statements and to show clearly their points of diversity or agreement, to condense arguments, to construct a clear narrative from disjointed memoranda, to explain shortly the main points of long reports, and generally to reproduce in a new, shorter, and more convenient form the gist of important documents. This will sometimes require much thought, power of arrangement, and skill in expression. Brevity will become more and more important, but so also at the same time will clearness and fulness, and above all things the most perfect inward digestion and comprehension of the whole matter.

With regard to expression, the precept to use as far as possible the original words will still hold good, but not to the same extent. Having satisfied himself that he thoroughly understands what he is to write about, the student should use the words which come to him most simply and naturally, being, however, very careful that he uses the words of the original whenever there is a chance of doubt. As to his composition, it should of course be grammatical and terse, avoiding all repetition and redundancy, ornament or rhetoric, long words or involved phrases—the plainest, simplest style that the writer can use. We might give the student exercises in terseness of writing and abbreviation of phrase, but, in addition to the reasons against this already given, the art of composition is beside the purpose of this work, which supposes that the student will have other opportunities of learning how to avoid tautology and other vices of style. It will be enough to impress upon him that this class of composition requires two things principally—(1) to understand what you are to write; (2) to write it in the fewest and best words.

It will be as well to begin our exercises in this section with condensed continuous précis of papers which the student has already read, and of which he has already made an ordinary précis.

EXAMPLE.

Give a short account of the negotiations before the recognition of King Alfonso, as shown by the correspondence, pp. 56–72.

When the Alfonsist Ministry was formed, Mr. Layard, the British Minister at Madrid, telegraphed to Lord Derby on the 31st of December, 1874, that he intended to act in his relations with them in accordance with the instructions received from Earl Granville on the abdication of Prince Amadeo. This course was approved by Lord Derby, who on the 26th of January, 1875, instructed him to maintain an attitude of reserve, while assuring the Spanish Government of the warm sentiments of goodwill with which this country was actuated towards Spain. On the 14th of February Lord Derby received a despatch from Mr. Layard, reporting his interview with the President of the Ministry Regent, in which the President stated that he appreciated the interest of Her Majesty's Government, and hoped Mr. Layard would soon be authorised to enter into more intimate and formal relations with the Spanish Ministry. On the next day Lord Derby, who had already received notice that King Alfonso had been or would be formally recognised by Russia, Germany, Austria, and Denmark, sent Mr. Layard a letter from the Queen to King Alfonso, accrediting him as her Envoy and Minister Plenipotentiary to His Majesty.

Exercises (G).

1. State, from the correspondence printed on pp. 75–80, between the Board of Trade, the Foreign Office, and Lloyd's, the reasons why both the Government and Lloyd's decline to take steps for the regulation of the loading of vessels with grain at ports in the Black Sea.

2. State shortly the misunderstanding referred to in the second paragraph of letter No 6, p. 78.

3. State the reasons urged by Messrs. Smith, Sundius, and Co., as given in their correspondence with the Foreign Office, printed on pp. 81–93, why H.M. Government should intervene to obtain from the German Government payment of their claim, and why H.M. Government refused to do so.

4. Give from the correspondence relating to the cession of Fiji, printed on pp. 94–118, an account of the part taken by Thakombau in the cession, and his opinions respecting it.

5. State shortly the provisions of the following portion of a Canadian Bill :—

Portion of a Reserved Bill of the Canadian Parliament, intituled 'An Act to Regulate the Construction and Maintenance of Marine Electric Telegraphs.'

Her Majesty, by and with the advice and consent of the Senate and House of Commons of Canada, enacts as follows :—

1. This Act shall apply—

(1) To every Company or association of persons hereafter authorised by any special or general Act of the Parliament of Canada, or under the provisions of this Act, to construct or maintain telegraphic wires or cables in, upon, under, or across any gulf, bay, or branch of any sea, or any tidal water within the jurisdiction of Canada, or the shore or bed thereof respectively, so as to connect any province with any other province of the Dominion, or to extend beyond the limits of any province.

(2) To every Company authorised to construct or maintain such telegraphs before the passing of this Act by any such special or general Act of the Parliament of Canada, or by any other special Act or Charter of any of the provinces constituting the Dominion and at the time of the passing of this Act in force in Canada.

2. The term 'Company' in this Act shall mean any Company or association of persons in the preceding section mentioned.

3. The Company shall not place any telegraphic wire, cable, or work connected therewith in, under, upon, over, along, or across any gulf, bay, or branch of the sea or any tidal water, or the shore or bed thereof respectively, except with the consent of all persons and bodies having any right of property or other right, or any power, jurisdiction, or authority, in, over, or relating to the same which may be affected or be liable to be affected by the exercise of the powers of the Company.

4. Before commencing the construction of any such telegraph or work as last aforesaid, or of any buoy or seamark connected therewith, except in cases of emergency for repairs to any work previously constructed or laid, and then as speedily after the commencement of such

work as may be, the Company shall deposit in the office of the Department of Marine and Fisheries a plan thereof for the approval of such Department. The work shall not be constructed otherwise than in accordance with such approval. If any work is constructed contrary to this provision, the Department of Marine and Fisheries may, at the expense of the Company, abate and remove it, or any part of it, and restore the site thereof to its former condition.

5. The Company may, in or about the construction, maintenance, or repairs of any such work, use on board ship or elsewhere any light or signal allowed by any regulation to be made in that behalf by the said Department.

6. If any such work, buoy, or sea-mark is abandoned or suffered to fall into decay, the said Department may, if and as it thinks fit, at the expense of the Company, abate and remove it, and restore the site thereof to its former condition, and the said Department may at any time, at the expense of the Company, cause to be made a survey and examination of any such work, buoy, or sea-mark, or of the site thereof.

7. Whenever the said Department, under the authority of this Act, does in relation to any such work any act or thing which the said Department is, by this Act, authorised to do at the expense of the Company, the amount of such expense shall be a debt due to the Crown from the Company, and shall be recoverable as such with costs, or the same may be recovered with costs as a penalty is or may be recoverable from the Company.

8. The Company may, with the consent of the Governor in Council, take and appropriate for the use of the Company, for its stations, offices, and works, but not alienate, so much of the land held by the Crown for the Dominion and the shore or bed adjacent to or covered by any gulf, bay, or branch of the sea, or by any tidal water, as is necessary for constructing, completing, and using the telegraph and works of the Company.

9. The Company may also acquire from any province of the Dominion any land or other property necessary for the construction, maintenance, accommodation, and use of

the telegraph and works of the Company, and also alienate, sell, and dispose of the same when no longer required for the purpose of the Company.

10. The Company may also acquire from any person or corporation any land necessary for the construction, maintenance, and use of the telegraphic cable and works of the Company, adjacent to or near the shore end or place of landing of the telegraph. And in case the Company and such person or corporation should fail to agree upon the possession or price of such land, the Company is hereby empowered to enter upon and take such land, limited to an area of five acres, under the powers, authorities, and provisions of 'The Railway Act, 1868,' the sections of which, in respect to compulsory powers for the acquisition of lands, are hereby declared to be applicable to any Company within this Act, and the powers, authorities, and provisions contained in the said sections of the 'Railway Act, 1868,' are hereby declared to be vested in and exercisable by any such Company for the purpose aforesaid.

11. The Company shall not be entitled to exercise any of the powers of this Act until the Company shall have submitted to the Governor in Council a plan and survey of the proposed site and location of such telegraph and its approaches at the shore, and of its stations, offices, and accommodations on land, and of all the intended works thereunto appertaining, nor until such plan, site, and location have been approved by the Governor in Council, and such conditions as he shall have thought fit for the public good to impose touching the said telegraph and works shall have been complied with.

12. The Company shall transmit all messages in the order in which they are received, and at equal and corresponding tariff rates, under the penalty of not less than 50 nor exceeding 200 dollars, to be recovered with costs of suit by the person aggrieved; and the Company shall have full power to charge for the transmission of such messages, and to demand and collect in advance such rates of payment therefor as shall be fixed from time to time as the tariff of rates by the bye-laws of the Company: provided, however, that arrangements may be made with the pro-

prietors or publishers of newspapers for the transmission for the purpose of publication of intelligence of general and public interest, out of its regular order, and at less rates of charge than the general tariff rates.

13. Any message in relation to the administration of justice, the arrest of criminals, the discovery or prevention of crime, and Government messages or despatches, shall always be transmitted in preference to any other message or despatch, if required by any person officially charged with the administration of justice, or any person thereunto authorised by the Secretary of State of Canada, or by the Secretary of State for the Colonies on behalf of the Imperial Government.

No Company or association of persons other than those mentioned in the first section of this Act, or which become incorporated in Canada under the next following section, shall maintain, construct, or use any telegraphic wire or cable connecting two or more Provinces of the Dominion, or extending beyond the limits of any Province in, upon, under, or across any gulf, bay, or branch of any sea or any tidal water within the jurisdiction of Canada or the shore or bed thereof respectively.

(Signed)   ROBERT LE MOINE, C.P.

OTTAWA: June 2, 1874.

6. Give a short narrative of the events detailed in the two following statements.

Declaration of Vice-Consul Magee.

That on the morning of the 23rd of April, about ten o'clock, he received a written order from the above-named Commander to appear at his Comandancia. Being unable to walk on account of a swollen foot which he was suffering, he informed the Commandant of his inability to attend, and requested him to excuse his attendance. The Commandant then requested him to make a statement in writing to the effect that he was physically unable to attend, which he did, adding that, as a Consular Representative of Her Britannic Majesty, he believed that any declaration that the Commandant might require from him could be made in his (Mr. Magee's) office, and would be considered valid, requesting this as a favour from the Commandant. That nothing more transpired until next day, when one of his clerks informed him that the Commandant had threatened on the pier to give him 200 lashes. That shortly afterwards M. Bulnes came to the office and stated that he was desirous of stopping the difficulties between the Commandant and Mr. Magee, to which he replied that he knew of no difficulties existing between them; that he had heard that the Commandant had threatened to lash him, and knew, from what he had seen, that he was a man of very violent temper, and consequently that, in future, he should carry a revolver with him in order to protect himself from being attacked. Messrs. Donnelly (British subject) and Villavicencia (Salvadorenean) were present during this conversation. About a quarter of an hour afterwards a Lieutenant of the guard with six soldiers, armed with loaded rifles and bayonets, entered the office with orders to take him prisoner. He told the Lieutenant that he was sick and could not go. The officer then begged him not to compromise him, as his instructions were to shoot him should he not comply and to take him dead or alive; upon which he accompanied the troops to the Comandancia, being carried thither on a car, as he was unable to walk. That, on arriving at the head of the Comandancia stairs, ten bayonets were presented at his breast, and the Commandant, seeing he was unarmed, sprang forward and presented a rifle loaded and cocked at his head, and with most vile, filthy, and insulting epithets ordered him to deliver the revolver he had in his possession. That he attempted to speak to him, but was not allowed to do so. He then took his revolver out of his pocket, which was immediately struck out of his hand with a bayonet, and he was dragged to the top of the stairs by violence, where the Commandant, using the foulest language, struck him several times over the head with his hand, whilst the soldiers pushed him into the Comandancia. On arriving in the Comandancia, the abusive language of the Commandant still continuing, a large revolver was twice drawn on him by the Commandant, who threatened to take his life. That he was then asked by the Commandant why he carried the small revolver, and answered that, knowing the violent temper of the Commandant, and the threats of lashes and personal violence which he had made use of towards him, he had carried it in self-defence, on which he was again violently abused by the Commandant and struck in the face with a revolver, and further threatened with death, a revolver loaded and cocked being put to his head. The Commandant also spat in his face. That after a short time, the Commandant's excitement having cooled, he was told by him that he (the Commandant) was aware that he (Mr. Magee) had injured him with the Government, and had threatened to assassinate him; the whole of which was politely but firmly denied, and he (Mr. Magee) begged the Commandant to reflect on the probability that he had been misinformed by persons ill disposed towards him. That the Commandant then stated that, whether he had been so misinformed or no, he had now gone too far to go back; that he hated him because he had declined to associate with him; that he intended to give him 500 lashes; that he intended to close the telegraph office, and that, therefore, four days would elapse before any interference from the capital could take place; that he, in that time, would flog him to death and would bury him; and that, when forces should be sent from the capital against him, he would resist as long as it was in his power to do so, and when nothing more could be done he would set fire to the whole place.

That he attempted to reason with the Commandant, reminding him that he was the father of a large family, upon whom his conduct would entail ruin and disgrace; but he answered that it was useless, as he had already ruined them and himself, and that he intended to kill him; further, that he had given a promise to flog him to death, and that he would fulfil it. That the Commandant then left him, placing sentries over him, and returned at the end of two hours and removed him to an inner and more strongly guarded room, where he was kept in close confinement until about three o'clock, at which time a German gentleman, M. Noltenius, was allowed to come into the room for a moment to speak to him on business, the Commandant being present. That the Commandant then told M. Noltenius that if he (Mr. Magee) had any business matters to arrange he had better settle them at once, as he intended to kill and bury him that same evening, stating further that he intended to begin by the immediate application of 500 lashes. That M. Noltenius expostulated against such treatment, but in vain. That shortly afterwards Mr. Edwin James, the American Consular Agent, presented himself before the Commandant and delivered him an official protest against all these proceedings, which the Commandant received, threw on the ground, and stamped upon, at the same time threatening Mr. James with personal violence, and stating that he respected no foreign Consuls. Mr. James then withdrew after attempting to make a verbal protest, which he was not permitted to do. That shortly afterwards all the entrances to the Comandancia were closed, the troops were called to punishment parade, and he was brought out by an armed force and marched into the common guard-room, where he saw the mats, sticks, and other instruments of torture lying ready, the guard ready formed, and the Commandant at the head with a large loaded revolver in his hand. That by orders of the Commandant he was immediately seized and stripped naked, during which time he protested against such treatment as a British subject and British Vice-Consul, reminding the Commandant that he represented Her Majesty's Government, to all which the Commandant answered that he might leave the Vice-Consulate to whoever he pleased, as he would leave his bones there in the guard room. That being overpowered by numbers (there being at least fifty soldiers present), he was thrown on the ground, and was held by a number of soldiers—about fifteen—kneeling on his arms and legs and on his head and shoulders, from the weight of whom he has received injuries in his chest, from which he still suffers great pain, and which may hereafter cause serious results. That he then received 100 lashes with sticks about half an inch in diameter and about four feet long, many of which were broken by the violence of the blows, the soldiers who inflicted the punishment being changed at every ten strokes in order that they might not slacken the force of the blows through fatigue, and several of them being themselves punished with blows for not striking with sufficient force to please the Commandant. That after 100 lashes the Commandant ordered the soldiers to stop for rest, and then sent for two glasses of brandy, one of which he offered to him and which he declined.

The flogging then continued, and about 110 more lashes were inflicted, after which the Commandant ordered the soldiers to desist, telling them they would continue flogging him in the morning. That he was again placed in close confinement, being suffering from the brutal treatment he had received, and being, moreover, covered with blood, and kept until morning without food. The surgeon of the troops applied once water and vinegar to the wounds, no other dressing being allowed. That at nine in the evening the Commandant entered his room and enquired how he felt, on which he answered, 'Very bad.' The Commandant then ridiculed him, telling him that he would feel better in the morning, as he would then receive 400 lashes more. The Commandant then called the Lieutenant and ordered him to send the soldiers to cut a fresh supply of mangle sticks for the morning. The Commandant then retired, leaving the room door open, and instructing the sentry that, should the prisoner move during the night, he was instantly to shoot him. That during the night the Commandant came twice into his room, once with a loaded revolver, and asked why he should not finish him ; to which he (Mr. Magee) replied that he did not know. That at six o'clock in the morning the Lieutenant came to his room and told him that the Commandant ordered him to get up. Whilst he was dressing the Commandant came in and ordered him to follow him, and that he need not dress. He was again forced into the guard room, where the mats, sticks, and other instruments of torture were again made ready. He was again seized by the Commandant's order, but in the moment when the flogging was about to recommence he begged the Commandant to listen to him for a moment, which was acceded to, the Commandant saying at the same time that, as they were the last words he would ever speak, he might speak them. He then led the Commandant aside, and begged him in the name of his family to accept 2,000 dollars and to allow him to endeavour to escape by running, even though the soldiers should make a target of him and shoot him while running, he being willing to lose his life by that means if by so doing he could escape the fearful torture of the lashes, and he feeling thoroughly convinced of the Commandant's intention to kill him by flogging. To this the Commandant replied by a refusal, stating that he had promised to flog him to death, and that he would keep his word. The Commandant then said that he would show him a telegram which he had received from the President of the Republic, and for that reason took him into the office of the Comandancia, where he (Mr. Magee) reasoned with him (the Commandant) and begged of him to release him and spare his life. Perceiving that the Commandant began to yield, and that fear of the consequences of his unauthorised brutality had taken hold of him, he followed up the advantage he had gained, reasoning with him for nearly an hour, at the end of which time the Commandant remarked that he thought he was losing his reason, and that if he (Mr. Magee) did not get out of his sight he believed that he would shoot him. The Commandant then pushed him into another room, telling him to consider over some plan by which he (the Commandant) might escape the consequences of his acts, giving him half an hour for reflection, and stating that he would reflect in like manner. In about twenty minutes the Commandant entered the room, and stated that there remained to him a choice of one or two ways, viz. that either Mr. Magee or himself should disappear from the country. That he (Mr. Magee) immediately replied that he would go, which was at once refused on the grounds that he (the Commandant) could not await the consequences of his past acts. That he

(Mr. Magee) next proposed that the Commandant should go, to which he assented, requesting funds for the purpose, and letters of introduction to his (Mr. Magee's) friends on the coast, all of which was agreed to, and by his (Mr. Magee's) request Mr. James, the United States' Consular Agent, was called to get the money referred to, and to conduct the Commandant on board the American steamer 'Arizona,' then lying in the port. That the Commandant then withdrew the sentinel from the door of the room in which Mr. Magee was a prisoner, and informed him that he would remain a prisoner until his own embarkation. That the Commandant then lay for nearly an hour in his hammock reflecting, during which time Mr. James constantly urged him to go on board, while M. Bulnes, an official of the Government, urged him not to go but to remain. That finally he resolved to go, and at once began preparations for so doing. In about half an hour, being ready, and before going, he sent for two glasses of brandy and requested him (Mr. Magee) to drink with him, which he, fearing to rouse his frenzy again, complied with, and after bidding one another adieu the Commandant started for the steamer, ordering the Lieutenant to set the prisoner at liberty. That being almost naked, he (Mr. Magee) could not leave the Comandancia until he received some clothes, and while waiting for them General Solares arrived, and immediately took command of the troops and possession of the Comandancia, sending at once a file of the guard to take the ex-Commandant prisoner; but as this latter had escaped on board, the guard returned without him. That General Solares then sent a demand to the captain of the steamer to deliver the ex-Commandant Gonzalez to the laws of Guatemala, but meanwhile this latter had arrived alongside the steamer 'Arizona,' where the passengers, infuriated at what had passed, refused to allow him on board, and on his attempting to ascend the ladder had shot at and seriously wounded him. That on his return to shore ex-Commandant Gonzalez was made a prisoner by General Solares.

I, John Magee, British Vice-Consul at San José de Guatemala, having heard the above statement read, do hereby declare that the facts and deeds therein related are strictly and implicitly true; and further I do hereby solemnly protest against all such brutalities, injuries, insults, imprisonments, outrages, &c., upon myself personally, as also upon the persons of any of Her Majesty's loyal subjects whatsoever; and further, I do hereby hold responsible for all such outrages not only the person aforenamed, but also all those who were instigators or participators of the same. In token whereof I have hereby signed the same with my accustomed signature of office

(Signed)   J. MAGEE.

GUATEMALA: April 30, 1874.

Declaration of Alexander Downie Moncrieff.

That on the morning of the aforesaid day the United States' steam-ship 'Arizona' anchored in the port, and he (Mr. Moncrieff) went off to visit her in company of an officer from the Comandancia; that, on the way on board, a boat from the steamer passed the visiting boat, and an officer from the former landed on the pier. In about an hour the officer who had landed returned to the steamer, and stated that he had been detained on shore by a guard of armed soldiers, placed on the pier by the Commandant, who intimated that the officer had contravened the laws and shown disrespect to the Government of the country by landing before the Commandant had completed the official visit. It was only after much trouble and the interference of the United States' Consular Agent that the officer from the steamer was allowed to re-embark.

Mr. Moncrieff then returned on shore in a boat belonging to the Honolulu bark 'Chocola,' in company with Captain Rugg of that vessel. On arriving at the pier, he learned that Commandant Gonzalez had given orders that none of the cargo of the 'Arizona' should be landed on the pier, and, after leaving the steamer's manifest and bills of lading in his office, he proceeded to the Comandancia to ascertain the reason of such an order. In the Comandancia he found Commandant Gonzalez swinging in a hammock, the Administrator Bulnes seated at his side, and Mr. Bromberger, a merchant of San Francisco, seated near the door. Saluting the company, and in reply to the questions of Commandant Gonzalez, he (Mr. Moncrieff) stated that, having been informed by the people on the pier that the Commandant had forbidden any cargo from the steamer to be landed, he had called to learn, and, if possible, to remove, any obstacle to the despatch of the steamer. The Commandant interrupted this statement, and desired M. Bulnes to explain it to him. Turning to M. Bulnes, Mr. Moncrieff proceeded to make the same observation in English, when M. Bulnes started up from his chair, exclaiming, with an obscene oath, that foreigners were not wanted there, nor any language except Spanish. He then went into an adjoining room, from which he brought a chair, and, along with the Commandant, invited Mr. Moncrieff to be seated. He (Mr. Moncrieff) begged to be excused from seating himself on account of the urgent necessity of his business requiring immediate despatch; and turning to Mr. Bromberger, requested him, in English, to inform the Commandant of the cause of his having presented himself. The Commandant said he had forbidden the discharge of the steamer's cargo because there had been no application made to him for permission to proceed with the same. He (Mr. Moncrieff) said that, if that were the only reason, he would at once remedy it by making the application, and was proceeding to state that, by a special agreement between the Government of Guatemala and the Steamship Company, such application was dispensed with, when Commandant Gonzalez started from his hammock, and with many obscene and abusive epithets, and shaking his fist in Mr. Moncrieff's face, said that he (Mr. Moncrieff) had for a long time been playing with and humbugging him (the Commandant), but that now it should be seen who had the power, and whether or not he could enforce his will with 'palos' (lashes) and bullets. He continued, ' As for your friend Magee, I will send for him now and give him five hundred lashes, and we will see if he will interfere with me again.' Mr. Moncrieff, turning to Mr. Bromberger, requested him in English to witness that the Commandant had threatened the person and life of the British Vice-Consul. The Commandant then went to the door, and calling his Lieutenant ordered him to take a guard and arrest Mr. John Magee, and bring him alive or dead to the Comandancia. 'If he resists, shoot him,' were his words. Turning to Mr. Moncrieff, the Commandant, making use of further obscene language, raised his hand to strike him; but, changing his mind, ordered him under arrest, and had him put in a room, giving orders to the guard not to allow anyone to communicate with him. Shortly afterwards Mr. Moncrieff saw a number of soldiers enter the Comandancia with Mr. John Magee in their midst, a prisoner. After an interval of a quarter of an hour Mr. Moncrieff was taken into the Commandant's office, where he found Mr. Magee and the Commandant Gonzalez. On his entry the Commandant took up a Deringer pistol, and holding it to Mr. Magee's head said, with many obscene and disgusting words, 'Magee, I am going to shoot you. I will give you 500 lashes and then shoot you. If anyone should be sent to supersede me, I will put a bullet through your head before I give up the command. They may shoot me afterwards, but you will be buried first.' The Commandant, after repeating similar threats to Mr. Moncrieff, left the room, and was absent about half an hour. During this interview Mr. Magee, in talking over the state of affairs, said to Mr. Moncrieff, 'I do not think they will touch you now, but may probably let you out. In that case try to communicate to Mr. Scholfield at Guatemala an account of these outrages.' Mr. Moncrieff asked, 'In the event of the telegraph office being closed by the Commandant, do you wish me to go personally to Guatemala?' Mr. Magee replied, 'No; I should like you to remain in this port. You have seen the beginning; I should like you to be present at the end.'

Shortly after this conversation took place the Commandant returned, and a young man named Santiago Villavicencia, a clerk of Mr. Magee, was brought into the room, and to him the Commandant made use of much abusive language, accusing him of plotting with Mr. Magee and Mr. Moncrieff to assassinate him (the Commandant). Mr. Villavicencia respectfully and decidedly repudiated the charge, when Commandant Gonzalez replied, 'I will allow you to go just now, but hereafter I will have you up and give you what I am about to give your employer—that is, 500 lashes and four bullets.'

Turning to Mr. Moncrieff, the Commandant said, 'I arrested you because the Company of which you are the Agent showed disrespect to me and to the Supreme Government of this country by sending an officer on shore before the official visit was made this morning.' Mr. Moncrieff defended the Steamship Company, on the ground of their having a special contract with this Company, in regard to holding communication with the shore immediately on the arrival of any of their steamers. He defended himself on the ground that he had no control over the officers of the Company's steamers; so that even had they contravened the laws of the Republic he could not be held responsible for their actions. The Commandant then told Mr. Moncrieff and Mr. Villavicencia that they were at liberty and might go.

Immediately on being released Mr. Moncrieff endeavoured to communicate with Henry Scholfield, Esq., Her Britannic Majesty's Chargé d'Affaires in Guatemala, but found that the Comandante had closed the telegraph office and placed a guard at the door. Mr. Moncrieff then sent off Mr. Villavicencia on horseback with instructions to telegraph from Escuintla to Guatemala advices of the outrages being perpetrated in San José. Having written a statement for the officer in command of Her Britannic Majesty's ships in Panama, and obtained the steamer's clearance, Mr. Moncrieff went on board the 'Arizona,' where he stayed about two hours, returning on shore about four o'clock. On the pier he met Mr. Edwin James, Consular Agent, United States' Army, who told him that Comandante Gonzalez had inflicted on his prisoner the lashes he had threatened in the morning. Mr. Bromberger, who was on the pier, said to Mr. Moncrieff, 'For God's sake return on board the steamer, as Bulnes and the Comandante have sworn that they would give you lashes as well as Magee, and that afterwards they would shoot you both.' Mr. Moncrieff went up to his office, and wrote a futher statement to Her Britannic Majesty's Naval Authorities at Panama, which was certified by Mr. James and two other gentlemen. He then begged of M. Noltenius, a German gentleman, to go out on the road, and should he meet any officer or force coming to Mr. Magee's relief, to advise great caution, as Comandante Gonzalez had sworn to shoot his prisoner should anyone come to supersede him. Having written to Captain Morse, of the 'Arizona,' requesting him to delay the departure of his ship till the following day, Mr. Moncrieff requested Mr. Donnelly (Mr. Magee's chief clerk) to take the note on board the steamer and to remain there until further advices. Having business of the Steamship Company to attend to, Mr. Moncrieff remained in the office till 11.30 at night, when he received a note from Mr. Magee as follows :—' Solares will be down in the morning at daybreak. Go out on the road and tell him he must be careful how he enters, as this fellow will shoot me as soon as he knows it.'

Fearing that M. Noltenius might have passed General Solares on the road, Mr. Moncrieff procured a horse and went some miles into the interior, where he waited till half-past six o'clock in the morning, when General Solares came along with M. Noltenius, and all then proceeded to San José, where, the General taking charge of the Comandancia, all danger of further outrage ceased.

Mr. Moncrieff here desires to call the attention of Her Majesty's Government to the fact that he had, two weeks previous to the outrages related above, personally warned the Chief Minister of the Government in the capital of the violent and unscrupulous character of Commandant Gonzalez, of his having assaulted a native of one of the neighbouring States (a clerk in Mr. Magee's employ), and of the serious results that would undoubtedly follow should such an outrage be attempted on any of Her Majesty's subjects, and he further holds the Government of Guatemala responsible for all the outrages committed on his person, inasmuch as that they were well aware of the very bad antecedents of the two chief officers—viz. Gonzalez and Bulnes—whom they had appointed to the military and civil commands in the port of San José.

And he further declares that, under Divine Providence, he and the other British residents in the port of San José owe their lives in the first place to the courage and prudence of Camilio Aceituno, the telegraph operator in the port of San José, and, in the second, to the energy and decision of Henry Scholfield, Esq., Her Britannic Majesty's Chargé d'Affaires for Central America.

I, Alexander Downie Moncrieff, having carefully read over the above statement, do hereby solemnly declare the same to be a strict and impartial statement of the facts as they occurred; and I do hereby protest against all such imprisonments, insults, outrages, abuses, &c., upon myself personally, as also upon the persons of Her Majesty's loyal subjects whatsoever. In token of which I have hereby signed the same with my accustomed signature.

(Signed) A. D. MONCRIEFF.

GUATEMALA: May 2, 1874.

7. State shortly the condition of the 'libertos' from the questions and answers in the following report.

REPORT BY VICE-CONSUL GIBBONS RESPECTING THE POSITION OF 'LIBERTOS' IN THE VICE-CONSULAR DISTRICT OF GUAYAMA, PORTO RICO.

Position of 'Libertos' on Estates.

1. When contract is made is a certain sum per diem agreed on ?—Yes.

2. If current wages become higher do 'libertos' derive the advantage ?—Yes.

3. Are they paid for overtime ?—Yes.

4. Is any difference made between them and other labourers in hours of work and general treatment ?—None. Hours of work from sunrise to sunset; no work on Sundays.

5. Are they ever ill-used or beaten or imprisoned by the employers?—No; the employers can do neither.

6. In any difference between employers and labourers, are the employers favoured by the authorities, and have the 'libertos' facilities given them to change their contract for just causes?—The employers are not favoured, but rather the 'libertos,' who are protected, and they have every facility to change their contracts for just causes.

7. Is food and clothing provided by employer compulsory on the 'liberto,' and are the deductions made exorbitant, or is the quality or quantity of the food deficient?—No; one feed per day is generally given, which is both good and sufficient—viz. cod fish and corn meal. No clothes are given. The wages are high—from 50 to 62 cents per day. They invariably get lodging besides on the estates free, and are paid overtime. Many also work by piecework, and can earn a day and a half pay in one day. They are preferred to the native labourers, as they will work on feast days, which the latter will not. Many make five dollars per week with overtime.

When the emancipation was decreed on the 1st of April, 1873, the 'libertos' were allowed to go altogether free; most of them left off work altogether, and only returned on the condition of exorbitant wages paid by the planters to get off their crop.

At first the system of contracting was much abused, unprincipled men without means contracting with a hundred 'libertos' and then allowing them to get their living the best way they could; but at the end of the first year all 'libertos' had to sign a *bond fide* contract with a responsible party, who was responsible for their good behaviour. There was no obligation for them to return to their former masters, neither was there any restriction as to what wages they should receive. Those who could not obtain a contract—generally on account of known bad conduct—were obliged to work on the roads, for which they were paid by the Municipality sufficient for their food—viz. twelve cents a day—and at night they were locked up. This they were obliged to keep up until they could obtain better work.

A contract once made is as binding on the contractor as the 'liberto;' in fact, it must be a very good reason on either side for it to be broken, the 'liberto' being favoured.

Position of 'Libertos' who have elected to work in Towns.

1. Are they obliged to contract in all cases?—Yes.
2. Are they well treated, and do they receive justice?—Yes.
3. What proportion of number work on estates?—Impossible to say, but very many who formerly worked on estates are now employed as cooks, house servants, &c., at wages from five dollars to eight dollars per month. Many of these, if well conducted, are allowed to have their own houses and sleep there.
4. Do employers of labour, as a rule, prefer 'libertos' or other labourers, and why?—In the towns employers have no preference; but on estates they prefer the 'libertos,' as they are strong and active, and accustomed to work every day, including feast days, which in this country are very numerous.

General Remarks.

1. Is there any idea that the contract system may lead to the reintroduction of slavery in fact, if not in name?—Not the least; it would scarcely be possible; at the end of a year the 'libertos' will be as free as anyone here, white or black; and now, so long as they behave themselves, they are not in any way molested.
2. When 'libertos' are fined by the authorities and, in default, punished by being made to work for Government, is any limit put on their term of imprisonment in proportion to the fine inflicted or the nature of their offences?—Yes, most certainly; they are generally imprisoned for a certain time and are paid twelve cents a day out of the public funds for their maintenance; or if they are put to labour their work would cover this amount. They are treated as any free man.
3. Are proprietors ever fined for transgressing the letter and spirit of the law?—Yes.

4. Do 'libertos' quite understand the terms of the contracts they enter into, or is advantage taken of their ignorance?—They quite understand the terms of their contract, which is in writing, and read over to them before the 'Alcalde' or Mayor. There is very little chance for anyone to take advantage of a 'liberto;' they know quite well when to claim the protection of the law.

5. Are 'libertos' and other labourers subject to private fines by employers, and is this system ever exercised to excess, so as to deprive the labourer of his wages to any extent?—No, but any 'liberto' coming late to work would not get any that day, and consequently no pay.

The arrangement of 'libertos' is good, as without it few of the former slaves would work; they all prefer to 'squat' and work one or two days a week to gain sufficient for their wants, which may be easily satisfied in this country, and for the remainder of their time sleep and lead a generally vagabond life.

Since the emancipation property and life are not by any means so safe as formerly, as robberies from houses and the person are now by no means uncommon, whilst before the emancipation they were very rare.

The gainers by the emancipation are, of course, the 'libertos,' but also the Government, who, up to the present time, have paid no indemnisation to the planters or former slave-owners. Government is to pay 75 per cent. of the nominal value of the slaves in a term of years; but to do this it will take from the planter in taxes 100 per cent. and make 25 per cent. benefit.

The rates of wages are exorbitantly high, and Government will not allow foreign labour to be introduced into the island; in fact, it does all it can to prevent labourers seeking employ from coming to Porto Rico by putting exorbitant charges for passports both on entering and leaving the island.

(Signed) CHAS. C. GIBBONS.

ARROYO, PORTO RICO: April 30, 1875.

8. Give as shortly as possible in parallel columns the remarks of the Secretary of State for the Colonies, and those of the Administrator of the Government of New South Wales on the five points specified in the Secretary of State's Circular.

The Secretary of State for the Colonies to the Officer administering the Government of New South Wales.

(Circular.)   DOWNING STREET: November 1, 1871.

MY LORD,—Questions having been recently raised in the Colony of New Zealand as to the powers vested in the Governor of a Colony to grant pardons, it became necessary for Her Majesty's Government to consider carefully the various bearings of this important subject; and I have now to transmit to you, for your information and guidance, the conclusion at which they have arrived.

The cases which have to be dealt with may be classed under the five following heads :—

1. Pardon of convicted offenders.
2. Pardon or security of immunity to a witness fearing to criminate himself.
3. Pardon of an accomplice included in a prosecution, and turning Queen's evidence.
4. Promise of pardon to an unknown person concerned in a crime, but not being the principal offender, in order to obtain such information and evidence as shall lead to the apprehension and conviction of the principal.
5. Promise of pardon to political offenders or enemies of the State.

With respect to the pardon of convicted offenders, a Governor has already full powers under the terms of his existing Commission.

I am not aware whether in the Colony under your government it has been the practice for the Governor to leave signed pardons in blank, to be filled up and used during his temporary absence from the seat of Government. But as the question has been raised whether this procedure is admissible, I may here observe, for your guidance, that such a course would be irregular, and I am not aware of any circumstances which could justify it. The Governor, as invested with a portion of the Queen's prerogative, is bound to examine personally each case in which he is called upon to exercise the power entrusted to him, although, in a Colony under responsible Government, he will of course pay due regard to the advice of his Ministers, who are responsible to the Colony for the proper administration of justice and the prevention of crime, and will not grant any pardon without receiving their advice thereupon.

When the person whom it is proposed to pardon has been already convicted, there can be no sufficient reason why the case should not stand over until it can be duly submitted to the Governor.

With respect to the second head—namely, the pardon of a witness fearing to criminate himself—it is undoubtedly necessary that means should exist by which the evidence of such a witness may be obtained. This case, however, may be better provided for by local legislation than by the exercise of the Royal prerogative through the Governor. The judge presiding at the trial should be empowered to give a certificate under his hand, that the evidence of the witness was required for the ends of justice, and was satisfactorily given; and such certificate should be a bar to all proceedings in respect of the matters touching which the witness has been examined.

With respect to the third head—namely, the pardon of an accomplice included in the prosecution and turning Queen's evidence it appears to Her Majesty's Government that no local legislation nor alteration of the Governor's Commission is needed, and the practice in England upon this point may properly be adopted in the Colony.

In England a pardon is not granted before the trial, neither has the party admitted as Queen's evidence any legal claim to a pardon, nor has the Magistrate before whom the original examination is taken any power to promise him one on condition of his becoming a witness.

In such cases where the accomplice's evidence has been obtained (which can be done either by his pleading guilty or by the Crown entering a *nolle prosequi* against him before calling him as a witness against his accomplice), and he appears to have acted in good faith, and to have given his evidence truthfully, he is always considered to have an equitable claim to the merciful consideration of the Court, which is usually extended to him by the Judge presiding at the trial, by the infliction of minor, or in some cases of a merely nominal, punishment.

With respect to the fourth head—namely, the promise of pardon in order to discover and convict the principal offender—Her Majesty's Government will be prepared, in future Commissions, to vest in the Governors of Colonies the power of granting a pardon to any accomplice, not being the actual perpetrator of the crime, who shall give such information and evidence as shall lead to the apprehension and conviction of the principal offender.

It is not, however, considered necessary to issue at once supplementary Commissions for this purpose, as you (or your Executive Council, if an emergency should compel them to take action at a time when you are absent and cannot be immediately communicated with) can issue a notice that the grant of Her Majesty's gracious pardon to any accomplice who shall give such information and evidence will be recommended. Such notice, which is similar to that issued in England in like circumstances, will have the desired effect, and the formal authority to grant the pardon can in due course be transmitted to the Governor by the Secretary of State.

Lastly, with respect to the fifth head—namely, the promise of pardon to political offenders or enemies of the State—Her Majesty's Government are of opinion that, for various reasons, it would not be expedient to insert the power of granting such pardons in the Governor's Commissions; nor do they consider that there is any practical necessity for a change.

If a Governor is authorised by Her Majesty's Government to proclaim a pardon to certain political offenders or rebels he can do so. If he is not instructed from home to grant a pardon, he can issue a proclamation, as was done in New Zealand in 1865 by Sir G. Grey, to the effect that all who had borne arms against the Queen should never be prosecuted for past offences, except in certain cases of murder. Such a proclamation would practically have the same effect as a pardon.

The above-mentioned are, I believe, all the cases for which it is necessary to provide, and I trust that this explanation will have the effect of removing, for the future, any doubt as to the exercise of the prerogative of pardon in the Colony under your Government.

I have, &c.,
(Signed) KIMBERLEY.

The Administrator of the Government to the Secretary of State for the Colonies.

GOVERNMENT HOUSE, SYDNEY: May 30, 1872.

MY LORD,—Your despatch of the 1st of November, 1871, marked 'Circular,' respecting the powers of a Colonial Governor to grant pardons, was received by Lord Belmore on the 25th of December, and immediately forwarded by him to the Cabinet. It was not returned here until the 18th of April—a delay occasioned, I believe, by other engagements of the late Attorney-General, whose report was desired as to the practice observed in this Colony.

2. Your Lordship's despatch appears to have been occasioned by some questions raised, and therefore, I presume, some difficulties felt, in New Zealand. With respect to the Governor's pardoning power, I am able to state that no question has arisen or difficulty been experienced in New South Wales; although, if we construe literally the terms of his Commission, difficulties might easily be made. The only questions which have arisen here relate to a different, although a kindred, point—namely, in what cases the Governor ought to consult his Ministers before granting or refusing a pardon, and how far, if at all, he is bound by their opinion.

3. Those questions have respect to pardons, absolute or conditional, after an offender's conviction, being the

subject which is classed, in your Lordship's despatch, under the first head or division.

4. With regard to the second, third, and fourth divisions of the subject (so called in the despatch), I have had a large experience in such matters, both as a Law Officer and a Judge; and I confirm Sir James Martin's statement that the English practice respecting pardons, or the promise of pardon prospectively, to witnesses and accomplices has invariably been adopted in New South Wales, as also, I believe, in the sister Colonies. The legal power of the Governor to pardon in such cases may be doubtful. Practically, however, no inconvenience has arisen, because the power of prosecuting is in all cases vested exclusively in the Attorney-General. Should a person ever happen to be convicted to whom a promise of pardon or protection had been held out by the Governor's authority, the pardoning power could then confessedly be exercised, as of course in such a case it would be.

5. On the class of cases fifthly specified, relating to political offenders and State enemies, no observation seems necessary, as no case of the kind, that I remember, has ever occurred in New South Wales.

6. I am glad to learn from your Lordship that the Commissions to Governors will in future be amended, by conferring in express terms the power of pardoning parties prospectively. At present (clause 6 in Lord Belmore's Commission) the authority given is restricted to convicted offenders. It will hereafter embrace, I presume, all persons 'guilty or supposed to be guilty' of any crimes committed in the Colony, after which I would suggest the addition of the words 'or for which the offender may by law be tried therein.' The power will then include cases of kidnapping and other offences in these seas, in which its exercise may be found of service.

7. By the Governor's instructions (clause 8 in those issued to Lord Belmore) he is 'in all cases' to consult with the Executive Council, except when material prejudice would be sustained thereby, or the matters shall be too trivial or too urgent to render such consultation advisable. Now, does this instruction apply to cases of petition for pardons or mitigation, where the sentence is

not capital? By clause 13 the Governor is specially required to consult his Council in capital cases, and not to grant or withhold a pardon until after receiving their advice. Nevertheless, he is to act eventually on his own deliberate judgment, whether the Council shall have concurred with him or not.

8. What is to be the Governor's course when the sentence was to imprisonment with hard labour (penal servitude) or to a fine and imprisonment, and the prisoner's friends, or sympathisers with his family, think the punishment too severe originally, or that he has after a certain period endured enough, or, perhaps, that the evidence was not sufficient, or that circumstances subsequently discovered or arising call for a mitigation ?

9. The practice hitherto adopted has been, almost as a matter of course, to refer petitions containing any such representations to the sentencing Judge. The consequence is—petitions of one or the other of these classes being numerous—that his time is largely occupied, if he does his duty by reporting fully, in (substantially) trying the case over again, and justifying his sentence to the Executive, or explaining why for the sake of the community it ought to be endured. I have always thought that these references should be exceptional—made sparingly and with due discrimination—and yet that the Governor ought never (or except under very peculiar circumstances) to mitigate a criminal's punishment without reference to and report from the Judge. In the majority of cases I am enabled to say, from my long experience, that these petitions require no such reference; but, notwithstanding the number of signatures generally attached to them, that they may summarily and most justly be rejected.

10. On this point of the subject I would refer, with approval, to Mr. Secretary Robertson's Minute of July 1869, of which a copy was transmitted to Lord Granville in that month by Lord Belmore, when asking for an official instruction whether he was bound, in deciding on such petitions, to act on his own independent judgment. Mr. Robertson suggested that the Colonial Secretary should, in every instance, submit his recommendation or opinion with the case, leaving its decision then to the

Governor. And Lord Granville, in answer, by his despatch of the 4th of October, 1869, seems to have (in effect) adopted the principle, observing that the Governor has undoubtedly a right to act on his own judgment, but that (in all matters at least of purely local concern) he ought to allow great weight to the recommendation of his Ministry. Your Lordship's Circular, the receipt of which I am acknowledging, appears to carry this instruction further, by the opinion, if not positive direction, that the Governor ought not to grant any pardon without receiving their advice.

11. It is necessary to state, therefore, what is (and, so far as I can learn, what always has been) the course pursued in this Colony: in order that, if it shall be thought by your Lordship to be incorrect or undesirable, a different system may be adopted.

12. The Colonial Secretary, in whose department all correspondence on the subject of crime, after conviction, is carried on, does not in the first instance express any opinion on a petition of pardon or mitigation. He may have done so in a few cases, but as a general rule he certainly does not. The mode of dealing with the petition is determined, and in effect all references concerning it are directed, by the Governor, a very considerable portion of whose time is occupied (I may say in every week) in the investigation of and deliberation upon such cases. Neither does the Governor, in general, confer with any Minister on them, although occasionally he asks the Colonial Secretary or Attorney-General to advise him. But, as the Governor's decision is always minuted on the papers, with or without his reasons for it, the Colonial Secretary, before acting on or communicating that decision, has the opportunity of forming an opinion for himself, and of submitting the case to the Governor for reconsideration, should he desire to do so.

13. In this way I submit to your Lordship the views expressed in Mr. Robertson's Minute, and in Lord Granville's despatch, although the order of proceeding is reversed, are practically observed.

14. It remains only to mention, that no such practice as that of signing pardons in blank, adverted to by your

Lordship, has ever (in, I believe, even a single instance) prevailed in the Colony.

15. Although it is not strictly on the subject of pardons, I would ask a reconsideration of clause 406 in the Colonial Regulations (edition 1867) respecting the Judges' notes in capital cases. The Royal Instructions accompanying the Governor's Commission require only that the Judge shall make a report of every such case tried by him, and attend the Executive Council when taken into consideration there, for the purpose, I presume, of affording further information if desired. The Judge accordingly does always attend, and he brings his note-book with him, reading portions of the evidence from it when explanation is asked by any Member. More than this, I submit, is unnecessary, and may even be embarrassing to the Governor. It is not impossible that the instruction referred to was intended as a substitute for the Regulation, but the latter, if in force, requires a Governor invariably to peruse the notes (necessarily, therefore, the whole) before decision; unless, indeed, he shall exercise the power of pardon, in which case it seems he need not read them.

I have, &c.,

(Signed) ALFRED STEPHEN.

PART III.
PRÉCIS-WRITING AS AN INTELLECTUAL EXERCISE.

CHAPTER I.

INTRODUCTORY.

THE art of practical précis-writing is to express in as few words as possible the sense of what you read, for the benefit of others; précis-writing as an intellectual exercise is doing the same for your own benefit. This in the case of the practical précis is done principally with the object of saving time, which would otherwise be spent in finding a document, or in reading it, but when done for yourself its use is by no means so limited. Of course what you have already done for others you can do for yourself, and therefore it would be useless to give to anyone who has studied the former parts of this work further instructions in the ordinary précis of correspondence; but there are many exercises in précis which, though of no direct use to others, may be of great value to yourself.

It will, in the first place, be of much use as *an aid to the study of composition*, for all composition is in a large sense précis-writing. That is to say, it should contain the fewest and best words for the purpose of the writer. Even in oratory—the most diffuse style of prose composition—too many words are as vicious as in an Act of Parliament. In the one case the object is not only to express what you mean, but to produce an effect upon your audience, and this cannot be done withot a profuseness of words, which would be unnecessary in the other, but speeches as well as Acts of Parliament can be spoilt by too many words.

Coleridge defines prose as 'words in their best order,' and poetry as 'the *best* words in their best order;' if he had added the epithet 'fewest' to both definitions, they would have been still finer, for even in poetry, which appeals to the emotions, and not (at least primarily) to the intellect, a word too much is as bad if not worse than a word too few. In letter-writing, again, in which garrulity is almost a virtue, prolixity and tediousness are vices of which we must all have had or will have some experience. The habit, therefore, of calculating the effect of the quantity of words as well as the quality will not be without its use in composition of any kind.

As *an aid to reflection* précis-writing will also be found of great value, for all of us are apt to read without thinking, especially if we read for amusement; and even if we think of what we read while we are reading we cease to think about it afterwards, and unless its sense is firmly fixed on the memory we lose it altogether. The habit of mentally reviewing what we have read acts as a check on the natural process of forgetfulness, and is the secret of acquiring real knowledge; nor do we know of any surer aid to this habit than putting down in a few words the gist of what we read or the impression which it makes upon our minds.

In this way it will become *an aid to memory* in the sense of training it to be watchful, and to make indelible mental records of our reading even though we do not have recourse to pen and paper at every stage.

Such précis-writing as this is also an *aid to judgment*, especially in regard to composition which, like oratory or poetry, appeals directly to our emotions; for though a fine poem cannot be submitted to such a process, any more than a bird or a butterfly can be submitted to dissection, without losing all its beauty, it is occasionally useful to test by such means what thoughts lie at the bottom of the beautiful words which have so moved us. In the case of fine poems it will rather confirm than destroy our admiration, and in the case of inferior poetry we shall detect the imposture of empty thoughts under sounding words.

The constant habit of finding the fittest and fewest words to express our meaning will also be of no little use in *conversation*, both in gathering the sense of others and giving form to our own, and we have no doubt that those who practise the habit will daily find some new use resulting from it, which we have not thought of or have not space to mention

CHAPTER II.

NARRATIVE.

A PRÉCIS of a narrative states in proper order the *events that happen.*

There is nothing that alters in the telling more than a story. The versions given by half a dozen persons who have read the same short tale in the newspaper of the day will be sure to differ considerably; and as the correctness of our judgment of events depends greatly upon the accuracy with which we remember them, it is of the first importance that we should habituate ourselves to make sure that we are correct both as to what events really happened and the order in which they happened. Whether words that are altered contain a definite promise or not, which of two persons first commenced an attack whether verbal or physical, whether a certain statement was made on the authority of a speaker or of some other person, are common instances of the numberless occasions in which the greatest confusion may arise from carelessness or inattention in reading. To ensure ourselves against such mistakes there is no exercise better than to put down in black and white the important facts which we read, even though the incidents are so few as to appear easily remembered.

In reading history and narratives of some length, whether truth or fiction, the habit is still more important. In reading a long story of any kind there are always many forces at work to make us lose sight of the main points. In history, digressions into minor issues, such as a small insurrection, will often lead us to forget some more important though less interesting event which we have just read, and when it is recalled to our memory we are unable to recollect where or when it occurred. In a story some surprise for which the author has intended to prepare us carefully is rendered unmeaning and unintelligible because we have not noted some incident told some chapters before. In all kinds of reading carelessness or defective memory will destroy much of its pleasure and profit, and the liability to both of these causes of error may be diminished, if not destroyed, by the custom of writing down an outline of events.

The value of this exercise for acquiring knowledge so as to be available when required is specially apparent in the case of students at school or college. Everyone who has tried to pass an examination satisfactorily must feel the importance of not only knowing his subject thoroughly, but also of having it at his fingers' ends, and nothing will supply him with both knowledge and facility to reproduce it so completely as the habit of précis-writing in this sense, for it is as it were a continuous examination of himself.

It is impossible within reasonable space to give exercises which will test severely the memory as well as quickness of apprehension and facility in composition. We cannot print, for instance, the third book of the 'Æneid,' and ask our students to give a succint account of the hero's wanderings, the places at which he touched, and the events that took place there; nor can we print the history of the reign of Charles I., and ask them to give a short account of the battles in which Cromwell was engaged, and the result of them; but the exercises which they have already done in Part II. will be a useful training for such more severe tasks, which can be easily improvised if required. The following exercises are intentionally short ones, and are given to train the mind to seize the important points of a narrative, to remember them accurately, and to express them clearly and concisely. They may also be made valuable aids to the formation of style.

When given for the latter purpose only, the student may be allowed to have the exercises by him for constant reference, but it will be more in accordance with the purpose of this book that only a certain time should be allowed for perusal, and that then the book should be shut before pen is put to paper.

It is also recommended that these or similar pieces should be read to the class once, twice, or more times, and the précis written without sight of the original matter. A day or more may sometimes be allowed to elapse between such reading and the writing of the exercise, which may be permitted to be the subject of discussion meanwhile.

A certain time should be allotted for the performance of these exercises, and the following is an example of the way they should be done.

EXAMPLE.

David Sands, the Quaker preacher, was exercising his functions in a family at Newcastle, as the Spirit moved, when, at the close of his discourse, he turned to the lady of the house and said, 'The mistress of this family will do well to set her affairs in order, for before twelve months are past the eldest daughter will be called upon to perform the part of a mother to her sisters.'

The lady was in perfect health, and, though this greatly distressed and disquieted her through the year, is living still after seven or eight have elapsed; and the daughter retains so strong and just an abhorrence of this presumptuous and mischievous fanatic that she has turned back from the meeting-house when she saw that David Sands was there.

In this piece the story is shortly and plainly told, and cannot be shortened without losing some of its effect on the reader, but at the same time the main facts of it can be stated in much fewer words.

It is plain, for instance, that the part of the discourse in which the warning was uttered is a fact of minor importance, and the reproduction of the exact words of the preacher, though effective, does not increase their significance. The state of the health of the lady at the time, her distress, and the approximate number of years she lived afterwards are comparatively unimportant in comparison with the fact that the prophecy was not fulfilled.

The essence of the story may therefore thus shortly be stated :—

David Sands the Quaker, when preaching to a private family at Newcastle, solemnly warned the mistress of the house that she would die before twelve months had past. The lady lived for many years after, and her eldest daughter retained such a disgust at the presumption of the preacher that she has turned back from the meeting-house when she saw that he was there.

Exercises (H).

Write in your own words, and as briefly and clearly as possible, the stories contained in the following passages, omitting all circumstances which are not essential. The student has in former exercises been recommended to use the words of the original whenever they will serve his purpose; in future exercises he should never use the original words, unless he cannot find others to serve his purpose as well.

1. Battle of Murat.

Murat.—I was told here that the Duke of Burgundy, seeing his army defeated, and himself environed, on one side by the lake here, and on the other side by the enemies' conquering army, chose rather to trust himself to the lake than to his enemies. Whereupon spurring his horse into the lake, one of his pages, to save himself also, leaped up behind him as he took water. The Duke, out of fear, either perceived him not at first or dissembled it till he came to the other side of the lake, which is two miles broad. The stout horse tugged through with them both, and saved them both from drowning, but not both from death; for the Duke, seeing in what danger his page had put him, stabbed the page with his dagger. Poor prince! thou mightest have given another offering of thanksgiving to God for thy escape than this.

2. A.D. 1753. Gloucester.

Here is a *modernity* (says H. Walpole—Letters, vol. i. p. 313) which beats all antiquities for curiosity. Just by the high altar is a small pew hung with green damask, with curtains of the same; a small corner-cupboard, painted, carved, and gilt, for books, in one corner; and two troughs of a bird cage with seeds and water. If any mayoress on earth was small enough to enclose herself in this tabernacle, or abstemious enough to feed on rape and canary, I should have sworn that it was the shrine of the queen of the aldermen. It belongs to a Mrs. Cotton, who having lost a favourite daughter, is convinced her soul is transmigrated into a robin-redbreast; for which reason she passes her life in making an aviary of the Cathedral of Gloucester. The chapter indulge this whim, as she contributes abundantly to glaze, whitewash, and ornament the church.

3. Victim to Apollo.

At Terracina, in Italy, it was an impious and barbarous custom, on certain very solemn occasions, for a young man to make himself a voluntary sacrifice to Apollo, the tutelar deity of the city. After having been long caressed and pampered by the citizens, apparelled in rich gaudy ornaments he offered sacrifice to Apollo, and running full speed from this ceremony, threw himself headlong from a precipice into the sea, and was swallowed up by the waves. Cæsarius, a holy deacon from Africa, happened once to be present at this tragical scene, and, not being able to contain his zeal, spoke openly against so abominable a superstition. The priest of the idol caused him to be apprehended, and accused him before the governor, by whose sentence the holy deacon, together with a Christian priest named Lucian, was put into a sack and cast into the sea, the persecution of Diocletian then raging—in 300.

4. *The Effects of Swearing.*

A gentleman had a fair young wife which died, and was also buried. Not long after the gentleman and his servant lying together in one chamber, his dead wife in the night time approached into the chamber, and leaned herself upon the gentleman's bed, like as if shee had been desirous to speak with him. The servant seeing the same two or three nights one after another, asked his master whether he knew that every night a woman in white apparel came unto his bed. The gentleman said, ' No. I sleep soundly,' said he, ' and see nothing.'

When night approached the gentleman, considering the same, laie waking in bed. Then the woman appeared unto him and came hard to his bedside. The gentleman demanded who shee was. Shee answered, ' I am your wife.' Hee said, ' My wife is dead and buried.' Shee said, ' True. By reason of your swearing and sins I died; but if you would take mee again, and would also abstain from swearing one particular oath, which commonly you use, then would I bee your wife again.' Hee said, ' I am content to perform what you desire.' Whereupon his dead wife remained with him, ruled his hous, ate and drank with him, and they had children together. Now it fell out that on a time the gentleman had guests, and his wife after supper was to fetch out of his chest som banquetting stuff. Shee staying somewhat long, her husband, forgetting himself, was moved thereby to swear his accustomed oath ; whereupon the woman vanished that instant. Now, seeing shee returned not again, they went up into the chamber to see what was becom of her. There they found the gown which shee wore, half lying within the chest and half without. But shee was never seen afterwards.

5. *Lady Grange.*

The true story of this lady, which happened in this century, is as frightfully romantic as if it had been the fiction of a gloomy fancy. She was the wife of one of the Lords of Session in Scotland, a man of the very first blood of his country. For some mysterious reasons, which have never been discovered, she was seized and carried off in the dark, she knew not by whom, and by nightly journeys was conveyed to the Highland shores, from whence she was transported by sea to the remote rock of St. Kilda, where she remained amongst its few wild inhabitants a forlorn prisoner, but had a constant supply of provisions, and a woman to wait on her. No enquiry was made after her till she at last found means to convey a letter to a confidential friend by the daughter of a catechist, who concealed it in a clue of yarn. Information being thus obtained at Edinburgh, a ship was sent to bring her off; but intelligence of this being received, she was conveyed to McLeod's island of Herries, where she died.—*Boswell.*

Lane Buchanan says it was supposed a courier was despatched overland by her enemies, who had arrived at St. Kilda some time before the vessel. When the latter arrived, to their sad disappointment they found the lady in her grave. Whether she died by the visitation of God or the wickedness of man will for ever remain a secret; as their whole address could not prevail on the minister and his wife, though brought to Edinburgh, to declare how it happened, as both were afraid of offending the great men of that country, among whom they were forced to reside.

'A poor old woman told me,' he adds, 'that when she served her there, her whole time was devoted to weeping and wrapping up letters round pieces of cork, bound up with yarn, and throwing them into the sea, to try if any favourable wave would waft them to some Christian, to inform some humane person where she resided, in expectation of carrying tidings to her friends at Edinburgh.'

6. *Incident in Nelson's Career.*

While the 'Boreas,' after the hurricane months were over, was riding at anchor in Nevis Roads, a French frigate passed to leeward, close along shore. Nelson had obtained information that this ship was sent from Martinico, with two general officers and some engineers on board, to make a survey of our sugar islands. This purpose he was determined to prevent them from executing, and therefore he gave orders to follow them. The next day he came up with them at anchor in the roads of St. Eustatia, and anchored at about two cables' length on the frigate's quarter. Being afterwards invited by the Dutch governor to meet the French officers at dinner, he seized that occasion of assuring the French captain that, understanding it was his intention to honour the British possessions with a visit, he had taken the earliest opportunity in his power to accompany him in his Majesty's ship the 'Boreas,' in order that such attention might be paid to the officers of his Most Christian Majesty as every Englishman in the islands would be proud to show. The French, with equal courtesy, protested against giving him this trouble, especially, they said, as they intended merely to cruise round the islands, without landing on any. But Nelson, with the utmost politeness, insisted upon paying them this compliment, followed them close, in spite of all their attempts to elude his vigilance, and never lost sight of them till, finding it impossible either to deceive or escape him, they gave up their treacherous purpose in despair, and beat up for Martinico.

7. Japanese Penitents.

Certain Japanese penitents make it their duty to pass over several high and almost inaccessible mountains into some of the most solitary deserts, inhabited by an order of anchorites, who, though almost void of humanity, commit them to the care and conduct of such as are more savage than themselves. These latter lead them to the brinks of the most tremendous precipices, habituate them to the practice of abstinence and the most shocking austerities, which they are obliged to undergo with patience at any rate, since their lives lie at stake; for if the pilgrim deviates one step from the directions of his spiritual guides, they fix him by both his hands to the branch of a tree which stands on the brink of a precipice, and there leave him hanging till, through faintness, he quits his hold of the bough and drops. This is, however, the introduction only to the discipline they are to undergo; for in the sequel, after incredible fatigue and a thousand dangers undergone, they arrive at a plain surrounded with lofty mountains, where they spend a whole day and night with their hands across and their face declined upon their knees. This is another act of penance, under which, if they show the least symptoms of pain, or endeavour to shift their uneasy posture, the unmerciful hermits whose province it is to overlook them never fail with some hearty bastinadoes to reduce them to their appointed situation. In this attitude the pilgrims are to examine their consciences, and recollect the whole catalogue of their sins committed the year past, in order to confess them. After this strict examination they march again till they come to a steep rock, which is the place set apart by these savage monks to take the general confession of their penitents. On the summit of this rock there is a thick iron bar, about three ells in length, which projects over the belly of the rock, but is so contrived as to be drawn back again whenever it is thought convenient. At the end of this bar hangs a large pair of scales, into one of which these monks put the pilgrim, and in the other a counterpoise, which keeps him in equilibrio; after this, by the help of a spring, they push the scales off the rock quite over the precipice. Thus hanging in the air, the pilgrim is obliged to make a full and ample confession of all his sins, which must be spoken so distinctly as to be heard by all the assistants at this ceremony; and he must take particular care not to omit or conceal one single sin, to be stedfast in his confession, and not to make the least variation in his account; for the least diminution or concealment, though the misfortune should prove more the result of fear than of any evil intention, is sufficient to ruin the penitent to all intents and purposes; for if these inexorable hermits discern the least prevarication, he who holds the scales gives the bar a sudden jerk, by which percussion the scale gives way, and the poor penitent is dashed to pieces at the bottom of the precipice. Such as escape through a sincere confession proceed farther to pay their tribute of divine adoration to the deity of the place. After they have gratified their father confessor's trouble they resort to another pagod, where they complete their devotions and spend several days in public shows and other amusements.'

8. *Robin Hood's Death and Burial.*

When Robin Hood and Little John
    Went o'er a bank of broom
Said Robin Hood to Little John,
    'We have shot for many a pound,
But I am not able to shoot one shot more;
    My arrows will not flee.
But I have a cousin lives down below;
    Please God, she will bleed me.'
But Robin is to fair Kirkley gone
    As fast as he can win;
But before he came there, as we do hear,
    He was taken very ill.
And when he came to fair Kirkley Hall
    He knocked all at the ring,
But none was so ready as his cousin herself
    For to let bold Robin in.

'Will you please to sit down, Cousin Robin,' she said,
  'And drink some beer with me?'
'No; I will neither eat nor drink
  Till I am blooded by thee.'
'Well, I have a room, Cousin Robin,' she said,
  'Which you did never see,
And if you please to walk therein
  You blooded by me shall be.'
She took him by the lilly-white hand,
  And let him to a private room,
And there she blooded bold Robin Hood
  Whilst one drop of blood would run;
She blooded him in the vein of the arm,
  And locked him up in the room;
There did he bleed all the livelong day
  Untill the next day at noon.
He then bethought him of a casement door,
  Thinking for to be gone;
He was so weak he could not leap,
  Nor he could not get down.
He then bethought him of his bugle-horn,
  Which hung low down to his knee;
He set his horn unto his mouth,
  And blew out weak blasts three.
Then Little John, when hearing him,
  As he sat under the tree,
'I fear my master is near dead;
  He blows so wearily.'
Then Little John to fair Kirkley is gone,
  As fast as he can dree;
But when he came to Kirkley Hall
  He broke locks two or three,
Until he came bold Robin to;
  Then he fell on his knee.
'A boon, a boon,' cries Little John,
  'Master, I beg of thee.'
'What is that boon, quoth Robin Hood,
  'Little John, thou begs of me?'
'It is to burn fair Kirkley Hall
  And all their nunnery.'

Now nay, now nay,' quoth Robin Hood;
'That boon I'll not grant thee.
I never hurt woman in all my life,
Nor man in woman's company.
I never hurt maid in all my time,
Nor at my end shall it be.
But give me my bent bow in my hand,
And a broad arrow I'll let flee;
And where this arrow is taken up
There shall my grave digg'd be.
Lay me a green sod under my head,
And another at my feet;
And lay my bent bow at my side,
Which was my music sweet;
And make my grave of gravel and green,
Which is most right and meet.
Let me have length and breadth enough,
With a green sod under my head;
That they may say, when I am dead,
" There lies bold Robin Hood."'
These words they readily promis'd him,
Which did bold Robin please;
And there they buried bold Robin Hood,
Near to the fair Kirkleys.

9. Part of a Report of an Enquiry into the Wreck of the 'Annie Verdin.'

The 'Annie Verdin' was a foreign-built vessel—American—drawing thirteen feet of water, registered at the port of Philadelphia, official No. 105250, and owned by the following:—John W. Hall, $\frac{1}{4}$; Harlesan Heekman, $\frac{1}{4}$; H. Verdin, $\frac{1}{8}$; H. Verdin, jun., $\frac{1}{8}$; George Saulan, $\frac{1}{8}$; S. S. G. H. Squire, $\frac{1}{16}$; and James H. Hubbard, the master, $\frac{1}{16}$.

The ship was three years old, having been built in June 1873, and registered A.1$\frac{1}{4}$ at the American Shipmasters' Association, New York.

The master has a certificate of competency (No. 5687) from the same Association.

The vessel carried a crew of eight, all told, including the master, and left the port of Philadelphia on the 9th of October last, with a cargo of coal, bound to Galveston, Texas.

Soon after leaving the port the weather is described as becoming blustery, with occasional squalls, and continued so for some days.

On the 18th the Abaco Lighthouse is passed, the weather being then fine. At about 10 P.M., however, of the night there was a change of weather, the wind blowing from the east-north-east, strong. Sail was shortened during the night, the vessel steering rather wild. A little while after, however, the weather improved and became again fine.

From the Abaco Light the course up to 5 P.M. was W. $\frac{1}{2}$ N., and at 4 A.M. hauled up a half-point to clear the bank at Sturrup's Cay, the Cay bearing S. by E. A course was also shaped to clear the Great Isaac Cay.

At 2 P.M. on the 19th the weather began to be threatening, the wind being at E.S.E., blowing a fresh gale, Gun Cay bearing north twelve miles.

It was at this period that the captain decided on running for an anchorage, and making a harbour until the weather moderated. The vessel was consequently veered, and at 7 P.M. the ship was anchored in five fathoms of water, Great Isaac's Light bearing N. by E. $\frac{1}{2}$ E. about four or five miles distant. A strong gale, but steady, was at this time blowing, wind at E. by S. Both anchors were let go, with sixty fathoms of chain on each anchor.

At 11 P.M. the wind had increased to a hurricane, and the ship began to drag. The kedge anchor was now let go, which had the effect of bringing her up for about an hour. At 12.30 the starboard cable parted, as also the kedge hawser, and the ship dragged off the bank and out to sea. After dragging for an hour and a half she was laid to under a reefed spanker with her head southward.

Between two and three o'clock the rudder-head was discovered to be wrung off, and to such an extent that the vessel became unmanageable. No land was at this time in sight, nor could the Great Isaac Light be seen.

At 11.30, however, a three-masted schooner was discovered ashore, on what turned out afterwards to be Settlement Point, the western end of Grand Bahama.

The captain's endeavours were now directed to keep his vessel off if possible, and to effect this set reefed mainsail, fore-staysail, and main-jib, and after shipping the cables tried to fill away.

The jib, however, was soon blown away; the ship became unmanageable, the rudder being of no service; and the vessel drifted in until she struck on Wood Cay Bar, near Settlement Point.

The captain in his evidence states:—

'When I saw there was no possibility of saving the ship, I cut the main and mizen halyards away, and let the sails run down on deck. Just before the ship struck I ordered the men in the rigging, as the best place for saving themselves. The ship rolled very heavily, the sea breaking completely over her. After being ashore for about seven hours the ship bilged and filled with water.

'We had one boat—a large yawl boat—quite large enough to have saved myself and crew.'

It is much to be regretted that while the men were in the rigging two of them, against the expressed wish of the captain, left their then place of safety, got into the boat, then tied to the stern, cut her away, and rowed off, with the intention, no doubt, of making for the nearest land. Under these circumstances this was a most dangerous proceeding. After a while the boat was out of sight, and fears are now entertained as to their safety. . . .

At 7 A.M. Captain Hannah boarded the wreck in his boat, he having seen her from the shore, and was some time after followed by his vessel.

The sails, rigging, and stores were saved by the crew of this vessel.

The captain and crew speak highly of the assistance rendered them by Captain Hannah and his crew, as well as of their good behaviour.

On the 22nd the captain and his crew left the wreck in the Bahamain schooner 'Matchless,' and arrived at this port on the 24th instant.

CHAPTER III.

THOUGHT.

A PRÉCIS of thought states in the fewest possible words *what is meant.*

There are many things which make it difficult to be sure that we understand what we read. In the first place, the reasoning may be abstruse and hard to be mastered without much private thinking, even though it be expressed in the clearest possible language. In such cases one must either give it up as past our comprehension or persist till we have thought it out, unless we take the third and more usual course—viz. of persuading ourselves that we understand enough of it for our purpose, and passing on to the next passage. This is a habit which should be most resolutely fought against, as it results in no true knowledge and leaves us with a mind stored with ill-defined notions, useless, superficial, and conceited. It would be far better to give up hard reading altogether, and confine attention to subjects and authors which, if intellectually of a lower grade, can be thoroughly mastered and appreciated. As long as we do this there is no knowing to what pitch we may in the end attain; the mind fed upon real knowledge will grow, and soon, it may be, the language which seemed so abstruse and the books which seemed so difficult will be found, to our surprise, to yield up their innermost meaning at the first effort. The boy who has read and persuaded himself that he understands Tennyson before his mind has grown sufficiently to do so thoroughly, will gain by his trouble only an ill-founded contempt for a less difficult poet, like Longfellow, and may possibly end his life without duly appreciating either; but he who begins with the easier author will be more likely to rise to the other and to end by duly appreciating both. But supposing that the difficulty of understanding an author is of this kind—viz. that it needs a strain of the mind to master the thought—the only infallible test that he has done so is the power to put it into different language. To help him to do this there is no better exercise than this kind of précis-writing—i.e. expressing the gist of the argument in a few words of his own. It does not matter whether you call it a paraphrase, or a digest, or an analysis; it is essentially précis-writing if it sums up in the most useful way the results of reading. We know no more masterly example of this style of composition than the late Rev. Frederick W. Robertson's Analysis of 'In Memoriam,' in which the inner meaning of each section of the poem is contained in a short prose sentence—sometimes of only two or three words and never exceeding thirty-five.

Another difficulty in the way of understanding is the style of the author. There is scarcely any style, good or bad, that does not present some such difficulty. Of bad styles it is scarcely necessary to say much to prove the point. Some writers tie up really fine thoughts in such knots of words that it requires patience to disentangle the true meaning; others conceal the poverty of their thoughts under immense heaps of words, and to those who do not trouble themselves to find out what the author means one class of writers will appear as delightful or as stupid as the other. On the other hand, there are writers the very clearness of whose style, if it does not blind you to what they mean, blinds you to the importance or unimportance of what they have to say. One is apt not to prize what is very easy of attainment, and to think that there cannot be much of value in thoughts written in very clear language; whereas, on the other hand, unsound thinking may be placed in such neat and pointed words as to put Reason off her guard and make us accept unchallenged an argument which is beneath contempt. These dangers, though they exist in all forms of literature, from the portly history down to little essays with which novels are padded, are still more to be guarded against in works of fancy and imagination, especially poetry, and for that reason many of our exercises will be taken from that branch of literature. Here Reason is naturally and properly off her guard. In reading poetry we place ourselves for the time at the mercy of our emotions, and allow them to be swayed with the music of rhythm, the charm of images, and all the seductive delights which a cunning workman can devise by the deft arrangement of words. So the chances of imposition are even stronger, and so are the chances of misunderstanding; for we read to be charmed; and the charm effected, the end we seek is attained. But yet, to say nothing of the after-effects of charging the mind with sensations uncorrected by reason, we cannot really be charmed as we should be unless we not only feel the power of the artist but also appreciate his motive. And to be sure that we do this there is no infallible test but the power of putting it into words of our own. Committing to memory is an excellent practice, but not for our purpose, and we would even say that, unless the process we recommend has been passed through in some way or other—i.e. unless the passage is thoroughly understood before it be learnt—it will be of little value to the learner, and be soon forgotten. Yet for some passages committal to memory is the best way to preserve them, because it is almost impossible to find words to express the thought so shortly and so beautifully as it is done by the author. Such a passage is the following, from Bacon's ' Essay on Death :'—' Men fear death as children fear to go into the dark ; and as natural fear in children is increased with tales, so is the other. Certainly, the contemplation of death, as the wages of sin and passage to another world, is holy and religious ; but the fear of it, as a tribute unto nature, is weak.' Even, however, in such cases as these the attempt to express the same thoughts in other language will be a beneficial exercise even though the result be a long and clumsy paraphrase, and we therefore append some exercises of the kind, although they cannot be properly called précis-writing, which, as before stated, may include paraphrases, but not if longer than the original.

We will now give an example of the opposite difficulty in précis-writing—viz. a passage where the author's thought is so poor and so confused that it is almost impossible to say what his meaning is :—

Of Fame.

There is a magnanimity in recklessness of fame, so fame
    be well deserving,
That rusheth on in fearless might, the conscious sense of
    merit ;
And there is a littleness in jealousy of fame, looking as
    aware of weakness,
That creepeth cautiously along, afraid that its title will
    be challenged.
The wild boar, full of beechmast, flingeth him down among
    the brambles ;
Secure in bristly strength, without a watch, he sleepeth ;
But the hare, afraid to feed, croucheth in its own soft
    form ;
Wakefully, with timid eyes and quivering ears, he listeneth.
Even so a giant's might is bound up in the soul of
    Genius ;
His neck is strong with confidence, and he goeth tusked
    with power ;

Sturdily he roameth in the forest, or sunneth him in fen and field,
And scareth from his marshy lair a host of fearful foes.
But there is a mimic Talent, whose safety lieth in its quickness,
A timorous thing of doubling guile, that scarce can face a friend;
This one is captious of reproof, provident to snatch occasion,
Greedy of applause, and vexed to lose one tittle of the glory.
He is a poor warder of his fame, who is ever on the watch to keep it spotless;
Such care argueth debility, a garrison relying on its sentinel.
Passive strength shall scorn excuses, patiently waiting a reaction;
He noteth well that truth is great and must prevail at last,
But fretful weakness hasteth to explain, anxiously dreading prejudice
And ignorant that perishable falsehood dieth as a branch cut off.

This appears to be meant for a comparison between genius and talent, or 'a mimic talent,' whatever that may mean. Genius is strong as a giant and confident as a boar. Talent is weak and timorous as a hare. One can afford to sleep without a guard; the other relies upon a sentinel. One knows that truth will prevail, and the other is ignorant that falsehood dieth as a branch cut off. It is quite impossible to make a précis of such a passage, because, despite its flow of words and wealth of metaphor, it is without meaning from beginning to end.

A frequent difficulty at arriving at the sense of a passage, especially in poetry, is that the words do not narrate the thought or mood of mind intended to be represented, but only indicate it. A poet in pain does not always say,

'I am in pain,' but he will say, perhaps, 'The sun is hateful to me,' or state the effects of his pain in some other way more or less indirect. As an instance of this we may quote Tennyson's beautiful song :—

> Break, break, break
>   On thy cold grey stones, O sea!
> And I would that my tongue could utter
>   The thoughts that arise in me.
>
> O well for the fisherman's boy
>   That he shouts with his sister at play!
> O well for the sailor lad
>   That he sings in his boat on the bay!
>
> And the stately ships go on
>   To their haven under the hill;
> But O for the touch of a vanish'd hand
>   And the sound of a voice that is still!
>
> Break, break, break
>   At the foot of thy crags, O sea!
> But the tender grace of a day that is dead
>   Will never come back to me.

There is not a statement in the poem which directly states the poet's meaning. He only bids the waves break, and states that boys are happy and ships sail to their haven, and sighs for a vanished hand and the tender grace of a day that is dead; the meaning which lies beneath and behind the utterance may be imperfectly stated in the following words : 'The one whom the poet loved best is dead; joy still lives for others, but is dead for him; the life of the world still goes on, but his part in it is over.' Such exercises as these, though not admissible under the ordinary meaning of précis, because the sense has to be sought for apart from the words employed by the author, may properly be included under intellectual précis, and some are accordingly appended.

The following extracts must not be taken as necessarily models of style or examples of just thought. The pieces are intentionally of unequal merit—for example, the two sonnets to the redbreast, one of which is an absurd conceit, the other a simple and natural poem.

Exercises (I).

Write as much as possible in your own words, and as shortly and distinctly as you can, the sense of the following passages and poems.

1. In works of art, think justly: what praise cans't thou render unto man?
For he made not his own mind, nor is he the source of contrivance.
If a cunning workman make an engine that fashioneth curious works,
Which hath the praise, the machine or its maker, the engine or he that framed it?
And could he frame it so subtly as to give it a will and freedom,
Endow it with complicated powers and a glorious living soul,
Who, while he admireth the wondrous understanding creature,
Will not pay deeper homage to the maker of master minds?
Otherwise thou art senseless as the pagan, that adoreth his own handiwork;
Yea, while thou boastest of thy wisdom thy mind is as the mind of the savage,
For he boweth down to his idols, and thou art a worshipper of self,
Giving to the reasoning machine the credit due to its creator.

2. There had been a heavy thunder-storm in the afternoon; and though the thermometer had fallen from 78

to 70, still the atmosphere was charged. If that mysterious power by which the nerves convey sensation and make their impulses obeyed be (as experiments seem to indicate) identical with the galvanic fluid; and if the galvanic and electric fluids be the same (as philosophers have more than surmised); and if the lungs (according to a happy hypothesis) elaborate for us from the light of heaven this pabulum of the brain and material essence, or essential matter of genius—it may be that the ethereal fire which I had inhaled so largely during the day produced the bright conception, or at least impregnated and quickened the latent seed.

3. He began writing for the stage most probably about 1591, and did not cease before 1612 or 1613. Now, one of the most decisive evidences of vigorous vitality is steady and healthy growth. In so opulent a nature as Shakespeare's one would say beforehand there must have been many capacities, comparatively latent at first, which only gradually exhibited their full energy as they found their due nutriment in a larger experience and a fitting sphere for their exercise in the demands of his art. His excellence, too, lies so much in the just delineation of the realities of human character and feeling, that without tolerably prolonged observation it could not attain its height. It should seem reasonable, therefore, to assume that his greatest works must have been the product of his mature age. But this conclusion, obvious as it appears, has not been received without question. Rowe, his first critical editor, propounded the notion that perhaps we are not to look for his beginnings, like those of other writers, in his least perfect works. 'Art,' he says, 'had so little and nature so large a share in what he did, that, for aught I know, the performances of his youth, as they were the most vigorous, were the best.' This whimsical paradox is part of the general way of thinking, which represents Shakespeare as a sort of *lusus naturæ*, exempt from the ordinary influences which mould and modify genius, and producing his effects by a kind of mysterious instinct, altogether apart from the general energies of a

powerful and comprehensive intellect. Johnson, with his usual strong sense, saw and exposed the absurdity of Rowe's idea. 'The power of nature,' he says, 'is only the power of using to any certain purpose the materials which diligence procures or opportunity supplies. Nature gives no man knowledge; and when images are collected by study and experience can only assist in combining or applying them. Shakespeare, however favoured by nature, could apply only what he had learned; and as he must increase his ideas, like other mortals, by gradual acquisition, he, like them, grew wiser as he grew older, could display life better as he knew it more, and instruct with more efficacy as he was himself more amply instructed.' In this passage Johnson, as it seems to me, attends too exclusively to the accumulation of materials, overlooking the spontaneous growth of the shaping and combining power. But, having regard to both considerations, we must expect to find the later works of the poet greatly superior, on the whole, to the earlier, in strength and splendour of imagination, in truth and breadth of painting, and in solidity and depth of thought.

4. The second essay is 'On Decision of Character,' a subject which the writer enters into *con amore*. He has evidently the highest admiration for this quality, and most forcibly does he set forth its inestimable advantages and the evils of indecision; so much so that anyone who reads the essay ought to read to the end, where the author shows that firmness, if wrongly directed, is but weakness in the sight of God. I give this caution partly because I know that there was in the world, even if there is not now, a certain school called the spasmodic school, which differed from the Byronian in this respect, that its disciples did not, like those of Byron, make heroes of mere passionate weaklings, but selected for the object of their worship one man remarkable for his strength and determination of character; if also remarkable for his badness, so much the better, because it seemed in their eyes to bring out his strength into fuller relief; and thus they would deify as a hero a man of whom we should be tempted to say, if we

met him in real life, that hanging was almost too good for him. But certainly Foster, with all his admiration for decision of character, does not pander to this spirit. He has, however, made one omission; he has noticed only the peculiar evils of indecision of character, and has failed to point out an opposite class of faults into which men of more resolute disposition are apt to fall.

Great decision is generally accompanied with a certain amount of doggedness, which will not listen to reason, which often brings its owner into trouble, and which prevents him from learning the lessons which his misfortunes ought to teach him. The directions which Foster gives to the undecided are wise and good; but there is one consideration which he has omitted to suggest which I think is a useful one for those persons to bear in mind whose indecision is connected, as it often is, with the fear of man. Probably one-half of those we meet with in this world are as great cowards as ourselves, and only require that we should make the first move (provided we do so with coolness and good temper) in order to induce them to give way. The very same persons whom it might be safe to oppose are often dangerous to run away from.

5. Deep is the sea, and deep is hell, but Pride runneth
   deeper;
It is coiled as a poisonous worm about the foundations of
   the soul.
If thou expose it in thy motives, and track it in thy
   springs of thought,
Complacent in its own detection, it will seem indignant
   virtue;
Smoothly will it gratulate thy skill, O subtle anatomist
   of self,
And spurn at its very being while it nestleth the deeper
   in thy bosom.
Pride is a double traitor, and betrayeth itself to entrap
   thee,
Making thee vain of thy self-knowledge, proud of thy
   discoveries of pride.

Fruitlessly thou strainest for humility, but darkly diving into self:
Rather look away from innate evil, and gaze upon extraneous good:
For in sounding the deep things of the heart, thou shalt learn to be vain of its capacities;
But in viewing the heights above thee, thou shalt be taught thy littleness:
Could an emmet pry into itself, it might marvel at its own anatomy;
But let it look on eagles, to discern how mean a thing it is.
And all things hang upon comparison; to the greater, great is small:
Neither is there anything so vile, but somewhat yet is viler:
On all sides is there an infinity: the culprit at the gallows hath his worse,
And the virgin martyr at the stake need not look far for a better.
Therefore see thou that thine aim reacheth unto higher than thyself:
Beware that the standard of thy soul wave from the loftiest battlement:
For pride is a pestilent meteor, flitting on the marshes of corruption,
That will lure thee forward to thy death, if thou seek to track it to its source:
Pride is a gloomy bow, arching the infernal firmament,
That will lead thee on, if thou wilt hunt it, even to the dwelling of Despair.
Deep calleth unto deep, and mountain overtoppeth mountain,
And still shalt thou fathom to no end the depth and the height of pride:
For it is the vast ambition of the soul, warped to an idol object,
And nothing but a Deity in Self can quench its insatiable thirst.

6. There was a certain Pisander whose name has been preserved in one of the proverbial sayings of the Greeks, because he lived in continual fear of seeing his own ghost. How often have I seen mine while arranging these volumes for publication and carrying them through the press! Twenty years have elapsed since the intention of composing them was conceived and the composition commenced, in what manner and in what mood the reader will presently be made acquainted. The vicissitudes which in the course of those years have befallen every country in Europe are known to everyone; and the changes which, during such an interval, must have occurred in a private family there are few who may not, from their own sad experience, readily apprehend.

Circumstances which, when they were touched upon in these volumes, were of present importance, and excited a lively interest, belong now to the history of the past. They who were then the great performers upon the theatre of public life have fretted their hour and disappeared from the stage. Many who were living and flourishing when their names were here sportively or severely introduced are gone to their account. The domestic circle which the introduction describes has in the ordinary course of things been broken up; some of its members are widely separated from others, and some have been laid to rest. The reader may well believe that certain passages which were written with most joyousness of heart have been rendered purely painful to the writer by time and change, and that some of his sweetest thoughts come to him in chewing the cud like wormwood and gall. But it is a wholesome bitterness.

He has neither expunged nor altered anything on any of these accounts; it would be weakness to do this on the score of his own remembrances, and in the case of allusions to public affairs and to public men it would be folly. The almanac of the current year will be an old one as soon as next year begins.

It is the writer's determination to remain unknown; and they who may suppose that,

By certain signs here set in sundry place,

they have discovered him will deceive themselves.

A Welsh triad says that the three unconcealable traits of a person by which he shall be known are the glance of his eye, the pronunciation of his speech, and the mode of his self-motion—in briefer English, his look, his voice, and his gait. There are no such characteristics by which an author can be identified. He must be a desperate mannerist who can be detected by his style, and a poor proficient in his art if he cannot at any time so vary it as to put the critic upon a false scent. Indeed, every day's experience shows that they who assume credit to themselves, and demand it from others, for their discrimination in such things are continually and ridiculously mistaken.

On that side the author is safe: he has a sure reliance upon the honour as well as the discretion of the very few to whom he is naturally or necessarily known; and if the various authors to whom the book will be ascribed by report should derive any gratification from the perusal, he requests of them in return that they will favour his purpose by allowing such reports to pass uncontradicted

7. O well for him whose will is strong!
He suffers, but he will not suffer long;
He suffers, but he cannot suffer wrong:
For him nor moves the loud world's random mock,
Nor all Calamity's hugest waves confound,
Who seems a promontory of rock,
That, compassed round with turbulent sound,
In middle ocean meets the surging shock,
Tempest-buffeted, citadel-crown'd.

But ill for him who, bettering not with time,
Corrupts the strength of heaven-descended Will,
And ever weaker grows thro' acted crime,
Or seeming-genial venial fault,
Recurring and suggesting still!
He seems as one whose footsteps halt,
Toiling in unmeasurable sand;
And o'er a weary sultry land,

Far beneath a blazing vault,
Sown in a wrinkle of the monstrous hill,
The city sparkles like a grain of salt.

8. After these two noble *Fruits of Friendship* (*Peace in the Affections*, and *Support of the Judgement*) followeth the last *Fruit*, which is like the *Pomegranate*, full of many kernels; I mean *Aid* and *bearing a Part* in all *Actions* and *Occasions*. Here the best way to represent to life the manifold use of *Friendship* is to cast and see how many things there are which a Man cannot do himself; and then it will appear that it was a sparing Speech of the Ancients, to say, *That a Friend is another himself*: for that a *Friend* is far more than *himself*. Men have their time, and die many times in desire of some things which they principally take to Heart; the bestowing of a Child, the finishing of a Work, or the like. If a Man have a true *Friend*, he may rest almost secure that the Care of those things will continue after him; so that a man hath, as it were, two Lives in his desires. A Man hath a Body, and that Body is confined to a place; but where *Friendship* is, all Offices of Life are, as it were, granted to him and his deputy; for he may exercise them by his *Friend*. How many things are there which a Man cannot, with any face or comeliness, say or do himself? A Man can scarce allege his own Merits with modesty, much less extol them; a Man cannot sometimes brook to supplicate, or beg, and a number of the like; but all these things are graceful in a *Friend's* mouth, which are blushing in a man's own. So again, a Man's person hath many proper Relations which he cannot put off. A Man cannot speak to his Son but as a Father; to his Wife but as a Husband; to his Enemy but upon Terms; whereas a *Friend* may speak as the case requires, and not as it sorteth with the person. But to enumerate these things were endless: I have given the Rule where a Man cannot fitly play his own Part; if he have not a *Friend* he may quit the stage.

9. *To the Redbreast.*

Sweet, social songster of the dreary hour,
   Whom Spring to flowering fields allur'd away,
   Now frowning Winter strips the fleeting day
Of all its blooms, and clouds portentous lour,
Retire, as erst, to Delia's sheltering bow'r,
   Humbly again for food to sing thy lay;
   And while the nymph that makes the moment gay,
Shall trill the lute, fraught with sweet music's power,
The notes, as to each cadence soft they move,
   With imitative skill shalt thou retain,
Till young Delight sports in the trembling grove,
   And verdure clothes the chequered vales again;
Then gladsome with thy acquisition rove
   And be the unrivalled warbler of the plain.

To the same.

When that the fields put on their gay attire,
   Thou silent sit'st near brake or river's brim,
   Whilst the gay thrush sings loud from covert dim;
But when pale Winter lights the social fire,
And meads with slime are sprent, and ways with mire,
   Thou charm'st us with thy soft and solemn hymn
   From battlement, or barn, or haystack trim;
And now not seldom turn'st, as if for hire,
Thy trilling pipes to me, waiting to catch
   The pittance due to thy well-warbled song.
Sweet bird, sing on; for oft near lonely hatch,
Like thee, myself have pleased the rustic throng,
   And oft for entrance, 'neath the peaceful thatch,
   Full many a tale have told and ditty long.

10. How soon hath Time, the subtle thief of youth,
   Stolen on his wing my three-and-twentieth year!
   My hasting days fly on with full career,
   But my late spring no bud or blossom showeth.
Perhaps my semblance might deceive the truth
   That I to manhood am arrived so near;
   And inward ripeness doth much less appear,
   That some more timely-happy spirits endueth.

Yet be it less or more, or soon or slow,
  It shall be still in strictest measure even
  To that same lot, however mean or high,
Towards which Time leads me, and the will of Heaven;
  All is, if I have grace to use it so,
  As ever in my great Taskmaster's eye.

11. Absence, hear thou my protestation
      Against thy strength,
      Distance, and length;
  Do what thou canst for alteration
      For hearts of truest mettle
      Absence doth join, and Time doth settle.

  Who loves a mistress of such quality,
      He soon hath found
      Affection's ground
  Beyond time, place, and all mortality.
      To hearts that cannot vary
      Absence is Presence, Time doth tarry.

  By absence thus good means I gain,
      That I can catch her,
      Where none doth watch her,
  In some close corner of my brain:
      There I embrace and kiss her;
      And so I both enjoy and miss her.

12. DUKE. So then, you hope of pardon from Lord Angelo?
  CLAUDIO. The miserable have no other medicine,
But only hope:
I have hope to live, and am prepar'd to die.
  DUKE. Be absolute for death; either death, or life,
Shall thereby be the sweeter.   Reason thus with life:—
If I do lose thee, I do lose a thing
That none but fools would keep: a breath thou art,
(Servile to all the skyey influences,)
That dost this habitation, where thou keep'st,
Hourly afflict.   Merely, thou art death's fool;
For him thou labour'st by thy flight to shun,

And yet run'st toward him still : thou art not noble;
For all the accommodations that thou bear'st
Are nurs'd by baseness : thou art by no means valiant;
For thou dost fear the soft and tender fork
Of a poor worm : thy best of rest is sleep,
And that thou oft provok'st, yet grossly fear'st
Thy death, which is no more. Thou art not thyself;
For thou exist'st on many a thousand grains
That issue out of dust : happy thou art not;
For what thou hast not, still thou striv'st to get;
And what thou hast forget'st. Thou art not certain;
For thy complexion shifts to strange effects,
After the moon : if thou art rich, thou art poor;
For, like an ass, whose back with ingots bows,
Thou bear'st thy heavy riches but a journey,
And death unloads thee : friend hast thou none.
Thou hast nor youth, nor age,
But, as it were, an after-dinner's sleep,
Dreaming on both; for all thy blessed youth
Becomes as aged, and doth beg the alms
Of palsied eld : and when thou art old and rich,
Thou hast neither heat, affection, limb, nor beauty,
To make thy riches pleasant. What's yet in this,
That bears the name of life? Yet in this life
Lie hid more thousand deaths, yet death we fear,
That makes these odds all even.
  CLAUDIO.   I humbly thank you.
To sue to live, I find, I seek to die,
And, seeking death, find life : let it come on.

  13. This is that which I think readers are apt to be mistaken in. Those who have read of everything, are thought to understand everything too; but it is not always so. Reading furnishes the mind only with materials of knowledge : it is thinking makes what we read ours. We are of the ruminating kind, and it is not enough to cram ourselves with a great load of collections; unless we chew them over again, they will not give us strength and nourishment. There are indeed in some writers visible instances of deep thought, close and acute reasoning, and

ideas well pursued. The light these would give, would be of great use, if their readers would observe and imitate them: all the rest at best are but particulars fit to be turned into knowledge; but that can be done only by our own meditation, and examining the reach, force, and coherence, of what is said. And then, as far as we apprehend and see the connection of ideas, so far it is ours; without that, it is but so much loose matter floating in our brain. The memory may be stored, but the judgment is little better, and the stock of knowledge not increased, by being able to repeat what others have said, or produce the arguments we have found in them. Such a knowledge as this is but a knowledge by hearsay, and the ostentation of it is at best by talking by rote, and very often upon weak and wrong principles; for all that is to be found in books is not built upon true foundations, nor always rightly deduced from the principles it is pretended to be built on. Such an examen as is requisite to discover that, every reader's mind is not forward to make; especially in those who have given themselves up to a party, and only hunt for what they can scrape together that may favour and support the tenets of it. Such men wilfully exclude themselves from truth, and from all true benefit to be received by reading. Others, of more indifferency, often want attention and industry. The mind is backward in itself to be at the pains to trace every argument to its original, and to see upon what basis it stands, and how firmly; but yet it is this that gives so much the advantage to one man more than another in reading. The mind should, by severe rules, be tied down to this, at first uneasy, task; use and exercise will give it facility. So that those who are accustomed to it, readily, as it were with one cast of the eye, take a view of the argument, and presently, in most cases, see where it bottoms. Those who have got this faculty, one may say, have got the true key of books, and the clue to lead them through the mizmaze of variety of opinions and authors to truth and certainty. This young beginners should be entered in, and shown the use of, that they might profit by their reading. Those who are strangers to it, will be apt to think it too great a clog in the way of men's studies; and they will suspect they shall make but small progress, if, in the books they read, they must stand to examine and unravel every argument, and follow it step by step to its original. I answer, this is a good objection, and ought to weigh with those whose reading is designed for much talk and little knowledge, and I have nothing to say to it. But I am here enquiring into the conduct of the understanding in its progress towards knowledge; and to those who aim at that, I may say, that he who fairly and softly goes steadily forward in a course that points right, will sooner be at his journey's end, than he that runs after everyone he meets, though he gallop all day full speed.

To which let me add, that this way of thinking on, and profiting by, what we read, will be a clog and rub to anyone only in the beginning; when custom and exercise have made it familiar, it will be despatched, in most occasions, without resting or interruption in the course of our reading. The motions and views of a mind exercised that way, are wonderfully quick; and a man used to such sort of reflections, sees as much at one glimpse as would require a long discourse to lay before another, and make out an entire and gradual deduction. Besides that, when the first difficulties are over, the delight and sensible advantage it brings, mightily encourages and enlivens the mind in reading, which, without this, is very improperly called study.

14. There was a time when meadow, grove, and stream,
   The earth, and every common sight
        To me did seem
     Apparell'd in celestial light,
The glory and the freshness of a dream.
It is not now as it has been of yore;—
     Turn wheresoe'er I may,
      By night or day,
The things which I have seen I now can see no more!

     The rainbow comes and goes,
     And lovely is the rose;

                The moon doth with delight
        Look round her when the heavens are bare;
                Waters on a starry night
                Are beautiful and fair;
        The sunshine is a glorious birth;
        But yet I know, where'er I go,
That there hath passed away a glory from the earth.

Now, while the birds thus sing a joyous song,
        And while the young lambs bound
                As to the tabor's sound,
To me alone there came a thought of grief:
A timely utterance gave that thought relief,
        And I again am strong.
The cataracts blow their trumpets from the steep,—
    No more shall grief of mine the season wrong:
    I hear the echoes through the mountain throng,
The winds come to me from the fields of sleep,
            And all the earth is gay;
                Land and sea
        Give themselves up to jollity,
            And with the heart of May
        Doth every beast keep holiday;—
                Thou child of joy
Shout round me, let me hear thy shouts, thou happy
    Shepherd boy!

Ye blessèd creatures, I have heard the call
        Ye to each other make; I see
The heavens laugh with you in your jubilee;
        My heart is at your festival,
        My head hath its coronal,
The fulness of your bliss, I feel — I feel it all.
            O evil day! if I were sullen
                While Earth herself is adorning
                    This sweet May morning;
                And the children are pulling
                    On every side
                In a thousand valleys far and wide
                Fresh flowers; while the sun shines warm,
And the babe leaps up on his mother's arm :—

I hear, I hear, with joy I hear!
—But there's a tree, of many, one,
A single field which I have look'd upon,
Both of them speak of something that is gone:
    The pansy at my feet
    Doth the same tale repeat:
Whither is fled the visionary gleam?
Where is it now, the glory and the dream?

Our birth is but a sleep and a forgetting;
The Soul that rises with us, our life's Star,
    Hath had elsewhere its setting
    And cometh from afar;
    Not in entire forgetfulness
    And not in utter nakedness
But trailing clouds of glory do we come
    From God, who is our home:
Heaven lies about us in our infancy!
Shades of the prison-house begin to close
    Upon the growing boy,
But he beholds the light, and whence it flows,
    He sees it in his joy;
The youth, who daily farther from the east
    Must travel, still is Nature's priest,
    And by the vision splendid
    Is on his way attended;
At length the man perceives it die away,
And fade into the light of common day.

Earth fills her lap with pleasures of her own;
Yearnings she hath in her own natural kind,
And, even with something of a mother's mind
    And no unworthy aim,
    The homely nurse doth all she can
To make her foster-child, her inmate, Man,
    Forget the glories he hath known
And that imperial palace whence he came.

Behold the child among his new-born blisses,
A six-years' darling of a pigmy size!
See, where 'mid work of his own hand he lies,
Fretted by sallies of his mother's kisses,

With light upon him from his father's eyes!
See, at his feet, some little plan or chart,
Some fragment from his dream of human life,
Shaped by himself with newly-learnéd art;
    A wedding or a festival,
    A mourning or a funeral;
      And this hath now his heart,
    And unto this he frames his song:
      Then will he fit his tongue
To dialogues of business, love, or strife;
    But it will not be long
    Ere this be thrown aside,
    And with new joy and pride
The little actor cons another part;
Filling from time to time his 'humorous stage'
With all the Persons, down to palsied Age,
That life brings with her in her equipage;
    As if his whole vocation
    Were endless imitation.

Thou, whose exterior semblance doth belie
    Thy soul's immensity;
Thou best philosopher, who yet dost keep
Thy heritage, thou eye among the blind,
That, deaf and silent, read'st the eternal deep,
Haunted for ever by the eternal Mind,—
    Mighty Prophet! Seer blest!
    On whom those truths do rest
Which we are toiling all our lives to find;
Thou, over whom thy immortality
Broods like the day, a master o'er a slave,
A presence which is not to be put by;
Thou little child, yet glorious in the might
Of heaven-born freedom on thy being's height,
Why with such earnest pains dost thou provoke
The years to bring the inevitable yoke,
Thus blindly with thy blessedness at strife?
Full soon thy soul shall have her earthly freight,
And custom lie upon thee with a weight
Heavy as frost, and deep almost as life!

O joy! that in our embers
Is something that doth live,
That Nature yet remembers
What was so fugitive!

The thought of our past years in me doth breed
Perpetual benediction; not indeed
For that which is most worthy to be blest,
Delight and liberty, the simple creed
Of childhood, whether busy or at rest,
With new-pledged hope still fluttering in his breast:
—Not for these I raise
The song of thanks and praise;
But for those obstinate questionings
Of sense and outward things,
Fallings from us, vanishings,
Blank misgivings of a creature
Moving about in worlds not realised,
High instincts, before which our mortal nature
Did tremble like a guilty thing surprised:
But for those first affections,
Those shadowy recollections,
Which, be they what they may,
Are yet the fountain-light of all our day,
Are yet a master-light of all our seeing;
Uphold us—cherish—and have power to make
Our noisy years seem moments in the being
Of the eternal silence: truths that wake
To perish never;
Which neither listlessness, nor mad endeavour
Nor man nor boy
Nor all that is at enmity with joy,
Can utterly abolish or destroy!
Hence, in a season of calm weather
Though inland far we be,
Our souls have sight of that immortal sea
Which brought us hither;
Can in a moment travel thither—
And see the children sport upon the shore,
And hear the mighty waters rolling evermore

Then sing, ye birds, sing, sing a joyous song!
    And let the young lambs bound
    As to the tabor's sound!
We, in thought, will join your throng
    Ye that pipe and ye that play,
    Ye that through your hearts to-day
    Feel the gladness of the May!
What though the radiance which was once so bright
Be now for ever taken from my sight,
    Though nothing can bring back the hour
Of splendour in the grass, of glory in the flower;
    We will grieve not, rather find
    Strength in what remains behind,
    In the primal sympathy
    Which having been must ever be
    In the soothing thoughts that spring
    Out of human suffering,
    In the faith that looks through death,
In years that bring the philosophic mind.

And O, ye fountains, meadows, hills, and groves,
Forbode not any severing of our loves!
Yet in my heart of hearts I feel your might;
I only have relinquish'd one delight
To live beneath your more habitual sway;
I love the brooks which down their channels fret
Even more than when I tripp'd lightly as they;
The innocent brightness of a new-born day
    Is lovely yet;
The clouds that gather round the setting sun
Do take a sober colouring from an eye
That hath kept watch o'er man's mortality;
Another race hath been, and other palms are won.
Thanks to the human heart by which we live,
Thanks to its tenderness, its joys, and fears,
To me the meanest flower that blows can give
Thoughts that do often lie too deep for tears.

15. The general doctrine of religion, that our present life is a state of probation for a future one, comprehends under it several particular things, distinct from each other. But the first and most common meaning of it seems to be, that our future interest is now depending, and depending upon ourselves; that we have scope and opportunities here for that good and bad behaviour which God will reward and punish hereafter, together with temptations to one as well as inducements of reason to the other. And this is, in great measure, the same with saying that we are under the moral government of God, and to give an account of our actions to Him. For the notion of a future account and general righteous judgment implies some sort of temptations to what is wrong; otherwise there would be no moral possibility of doing wrong, nor ground for judgment or discrimination. But there is this difference, that the word 'probation' is more distinctly and particularly expressive of allurements to wrong, or difficulties in adhering uniformly to what is right, and of the danger of miscarrying by such temptations, than the words 'moral government.' A state of probation, then, as thus particularly implying in it trial, difficulties, and danger, may require to be considered distinctly by itself.

And as the moral government of God, which religion teaches us, implies that we are in a state of trial with regard to a future world, so also His natural government over us implies that we are in a state of trial, in the like sense, with regard to the present world. Natural government by rewards and punishments as much implies natural trial as moral government does moral trial. The natural government of God, here meant, consists in His annexing pleasure to some actions, and pain to others, which are in our power to do or forbear, and in giving us notice of such appointment beforehand. This necessarily implies that He has made our happiness and misery, or our interest, to depend in part upon ourselves. And so far as men have temptations to any course of action, which will probably occasion them greater temporal inconvenience and uneasiness than satisfaction, so far their temporal interest is in danger from themselves, or they are in a state of trial with respect to it. Now, people often blame others, and even themselves, for their misconduct in their temporal concerns. And we find many are greatly wanting to themselves, and miss of that natural happiness which they might have obtained in the present life; perhaps everyone does in some degree. But many run themselves into great inconvenience, and into extreme distress and misery, not through incapacity of knowing better and doing better for themselves, which would be nothing to the present purpose, but through their own fault. And these things necessarily imply temptation, and danger of miscarrying, in a greater or less degree, with respect to our worldly interest or happiness. Everyone too, without having religion in his thoughts, speaks of the hazards which young people run upon their setting out in the world—hazards from other causes than merely their ignorance and unavoidable accidents. And some courses of vice at least being contrary to men's worldly interest or good, temptations to these must at the same time be temptations to forego our present and our future interest. Thus in our natural or temporal capacity we are in a state of trial—i.e. of difficulty and danger—analogous or like to our moral and religious trial.

CIVIL SERVICE HANDBOOKS.

Indispensable for Candidates for Examinations.

The ESSAY WRITER: *being Hints on Essays and* How to Write Them. With Outlines of Eighty Essays, Designed for Examination Candidates, Public Schools, and Students generally. By HENRY SKIPTON. Second Edition. Fcp. 8vo. 2s. 6d. cloth.

'The book is altogether a good one.'—SCHOOLMASTER.
'Invaluable to those preparing for examinations in which essays are an element.'
CIVIL SERVICE GAZETTE.

The PRÉCIS BOOK; *or, Lessons in Accuracy of State-*ment and Preciseness of Expression. For Civil Service Students, Self-Education, and use in Schools. By W. COSMO MONKHOUSE, of the Board of Trade. Fifth Edition. Fcp. 8vo. cloth, 2s. 6d. KEY, 2s. 6d. cloth.

'Mr. Monkhouse has done intending candidates for appointments under the Crown real service. The examples given and the hints and suggestions are all excellent.'—CIVIL SERVICE GAZETTE.

The CIVIL SERVICE COACH: *a Practical Exposition* of the Civil Service Curriculum, and Guide to the Lower Division of the Service and its competitive Examinations. By STANLEY SAVILL, of H.M. Civil Service. New Edition, Revised. Fcp. 8vo. 2s. 6d cloth.

'Gives many valuable hints and much good advice.'—ATHENÆUM.

The CIVIL SERVICE GEOGRAPHY, *General and* Political. By L. M. D. SPENCE. Revised by the late THOMAS GRAY, of the Board of Trade. Tenth Edition, Woodcuts and Six Maps, fcp. 2s. 6d. cloth.

'A thoroughly reliable as well as a most ingenious compendium of geography.'
CIVIL SERVICE GAZETTE.

The CIVIL SERVICE HISTORY *of* ENGLAND: *being a* Fact-Book of English History. By F. A. WHITE, B.A. Seventh Edition, Revised, Corrected and Enlarged by H. A. DOBSON, Board of Trade. 2s. 6d. cloth.

'We do not remember to have seen anything of the kind so compendious, complete, accurate, and convenient for use.'—ATHENÆUM.

The CIVIL SERVICE FIRST FRENCH BOOK: *being a* Practical First Course of French Grammar, with Exercises combined. By ACHILLE MOTTEAU. Second Edition, fcp. 1s. 6d. *** KEY to same, 2s. 6d.

The CIVIL SERVICE ENGLISH GRAMMAR: *being* Notes on the History and Grammar of the English Language. By W. V. YATES. New Edition, Revised and Enlarged, fcp. 1s. 6d. cloth.

'We cannot call to mind any single work which would render so much assistance as is offered here to the student preparing to undergo examination in Grammar and Language.'—THE SCHOOL BOARD CHRONICLE.

The CIVIL SERVICE BOOK-KEEPING; *or, Book-*Keeping no Mystery. Its Principles Popularly Explained, and the Theory of Double Entry Analysed. Fifth Edition, fcp. 1s. 6d. cloth.

'It is clear and concise, and exactly such a text-book as students require.'
QUARTERLY JOURNAL OF EDUCATION.

The CIVIL SERVICE CHRONOLOGY *of* HISTORY, ART, LITERATURE, and PROGRESS. By W. D. HAMILTON. Fcp. 3s. 6d. cloth.

'Accurate, wide, and thorough. Most useful to those who are reading up for examinations.'—ENGLISH CHURCHMAN.

CROSBY LOCKWOOD & SON, 7 Stationers'-Hall Court, E.C.

STANDARD EDUCATIONAL BOOKS

PUBLISHED BY

CROSBY LOCKWOOD & SON,

7, STATIONERS' HALL COURT, LONDON, E.C.

NEW BOOK OF COMMERCIAL FRENCH: Grammar, Vocabulary, Correspondence, Commercial Documents, Geography, Arithmetic, Lexicon. By P. CARROUÉ, Professor in the City High School, J.-B. Say (Paris). Crown 8vo, 4s. 6d. cloth. [*Just published*.

"An excellent manual for those completing their French studies and entering a commercial career."—*Saturday Review.*

"Nothing better could be desired. It is a *vade mecum* of commercial French, and would be distinctly in its place in every merchant's office."—*Educational Times.*

"Those who have a mercantile career in view will find this compendious yet complete book well adapted to secure success in the study of the French language for such a purpose."—*Educational News.*

LESSONS IN COMMERCE. By Professor R. GAMBARO, of the Royal High Commercial School at Genoa. Edited and Revised by JAMES GAULT, Professor of Commerce and Commercial Law in King's College, London. Second Edition, Revised. Crown 8vo, 3s. 6d. cloth.

"The publishers of this work have rendered considerable service to the cause of commercial education by the opportune production of this volume."—*Chamber of Commerce Journal.*

"An invaluable guide in the hands of those who are preparing for a commercial career, and, in fact, the information it contains on matters of business should be impressed on every one."—*Counting House.*

THE FOREIGN COMMERCIAL CORRESPONDENT: Being Aids to Commercial Correspondence in Five Languages— ENGLISH, GERMAN, FRENCH, ITALIAN and SPANISH. Containing Forms of Correspondence such as are required for daily use in a Merchant's Office. By C. E. BAKER. Second Edition, Revised. Crown 8vo, 3s. 6d., cloth.

"If a good use is made of this book the student will very soon have sufficient knowledge to fit him for conducting such a correspondence in these languages as is required by ordinary commercial routine."—*Civil Service Gazette.*

"An English student, bent on success in his business life, will find this volume his vade-mecum."—*Publishers' Circular.*

A HANDY BOOK OF ENGLISH SPELLING. With ample Rules and carefully arranged Exercises. Adapted for the use of Schools, and of Candidates for the Services. By E. S. H. BAGNOLD. Third Edition, Revised. Fcap. 8vo, 1s. 3d. cloth.

"A very handy, carefully written, and complete little book."—*Pall Mall Gazette.*

DR. DE FIVAS' FRENCH CLASS BOOKS.

'The works of M. de Fivas are among the best that we possess for the means of acquiring a knowledge of the French language. If any proof were needed of this assertion, we should only have to point to the fact that they have gone through so many editions and still retain their popularity. This is a certain index to real worth.'
— CIVIL SERVICE GAZETTE.

DE FIVAS' NEW GRAMMAR OF FRENCH GRAMMARS;

comprising the substance of all the most approved French Grammars extant, but more especially of the standard work 'La Grammaire des Grammaires;' sanctioned by the French Academy and the University of Paris. With numerous Exercises and Examples illustrative of every Rule. By DR. V. DE FIVAS, M.A., F.E.I.S., Member of the Grammatical Society of Paris, &c. &c. Fifty-third Edition, Revised and Enlarged. With an Appendix on the HISTORY AND ETYMOLOGY OF THE FRENCH LANGUAGE. 2s. 6d. strongly bound.

*** KEY to the same, 3s. 6d. bound.

'The addition of an Appendix on the History of the French Language, compiled from the best authorities, gives a new value to this old-established school book.'—ATHENÆUM.
'The best and most complete grammar of the French language ever prepared for the use of English students.'—SCOTSMAN.
'It would be difficult to name a grammar better suited for instilling a sound knowledge of the French language.'—SCHOOLMASTER.

DE FIVAS' ELEMENTARY FRENCH GRAMMAR: based

upon the Accidence of the 'New Grammar of French Grammars.' By DR. V. DE FIVAS, M.A., F.E.I.S. To which is added a FRENCH READER; or, Selections in Prose and Verse from Standard Authors, with a FRENCH-ENGLISH VOCABULARY of all the Words used. Fourth Edition. revised. Fcap. 8vo, price 1s. 6d. strongly bound.

☞ *Intended to prepare the younger students and Junior Classes for the study of the more advanced work.*

'The elementary rules of the subject are explained in a clear and coherent system, and the main work is supplemented by a selection of extracts in prose and verse admirably well adapted for the study of junior classes.'—SCOTSMAN.
'One of the particularly good points in this little book is the full and clear manner in which the irregular verbs are conjugated.'—SCHOOLMASTER.
'As a thoroughly practical and workmanlike text-book we give it our warmest recommendation.'—TEACHERS' AID.

DE FIVAS' NEW GUIDE TO MODERN FRENCH CON-

VERSATION; or, The Student and Tourist's French Vade-Mecum; containing a Comprehensive Vocabulary, and Phrases and Dialogues; with Models of Letters, Notes, and Cards; Comparative Tables of the British and French Coins, Weights and Measures, &c. Thirty second Ed. thoroughly revised, 18mo, 2s. 6d. strongly half-bound.

'Has the advantage over other French conversation books of indicating the *liaisons* and giving other helps to pronunciation.'—ACADEMY.
'Compiled with great labour and care, and modernised down to the latest changes in the custom of ordinary French speech.'—SCHOOL BOARD CHRONICLE.

DE FIVAS, INTRODUCTION À LA LANGUE FRAN-

ÇAISE; ou, Fables et Contes Choisis; Anecdotes Instructives, Faits Mémorables, &c. Avec un Dictionnaire de tous les Mots traduits en Anglais. À l'usage de la jeunesse, et de ceux qui commencent à apprendre la langue Francaise. Twenty-eighth Edition, 2s. 6d. bound.

'By far the best first French reading-book, whether for schools or adult pupils.'— TAIT'S MAGAZINE.
'We strongly advise students to read this excellent book, and they will soon find their knowledge of the language enlarged and, to a great extent, perfected.'—PUBLIC OPINION.

DE FIVAS, BEAUTÉS DES ÉCRIVAINS FRANÇAIS,

Anciens et Modernes. Quinzième Édition, augmentée de Notes Historiques, Géographiques, Philosophiques, Littéraires, Grammaticales et Biographiques. 2s. 6d. bound.

'A convenient reading-book for the student of the French language, at the same time affording a pleasing and interesting view of French literature.'—OBSERVER.

DE FIVAS, LE TRÉSOR NATIONAL; or, Guide to the

Translation of English into French at sight. Seventh Edition, 1s. 6d. bound. (A KEY to the same, 2s.)

LOCKWOOD'S CIVIL SERVICE HANDBOOKS.

THE ESSAY WRITER: being Hints on Essays and How to Write Them. With Outlines of Eighty Essays. Designed for Examination Candidates, Public Schools, and Students generally. By HENRY SKIPTON. Second Edition. Fcp. 8vo, 2s. 6d., cloth.

'The outlines present a great variety and a judicious selection of subjects. The introductory remarks are much to the point, and the book is altogether a good one.'—SCHOOLMASTER.

'To those preparing for examinations in which essays are an element, this work will prove invaluable.'—CIVIL SERVICE GAZETTE.

THE PRÉCIS BOOK; or, Lessons in Accuracy of Statement and Preciseness of Expression. For Civil Service Students, Self-Education, and use in Schools. By W. COSMO MONKHOUSE, of the Board of Trade. New Edition. Fcp. 2s. 6d. cloth. (A KEY to the same, 2s. 6d. cloth).

'Mr. Monkhouse has done intending candidates for appointments under the Crown real service. It is an excellent book.'—CIVIL SERVICE GAZETTE.

THE CIVIL SERVICE COACH: a Practical Exposition of the Civil Service Curriculum, and Guide to the Lower Division of the Service and its Competitive Examinations. By STANLEY SAVILL, of H.M. Civil Service. Second Edition, Revised. Fcp. 8vo, 2s. 6d. cloth.

Gives many valuable hints and much good advice.'—ATHENÆUM.

A HANDBOOK OF ENGLISH LITERATURE. By H. A. DOBSON, Board of Trade. Second Edition. Fcp. 3s. 6d. cloth.

'For truth of criticism it is about the best book of the kind.'—WESTMINSTER REVIEW.
'An excellent hand-book of English Literature.'—ATHENÆUM.

THE CIVIL SERVICE GEOGRAPHY, General and Political. By L. M. D. SPENCE. Revised by THOMAS GRAY, of the Board of Trade. Tenth Edition, Revised and Corrected. With Six Maps. Fcp. 2s. 6d. cloth.

'A good manual for practical purposes, adapted to the present state of knowledge. The most recent political changes of territory are noticed, and the latest statistics inserted from authoritative sources.'—ATHENÆUM.

THE CIVIL SERVICE HISTORY OF ENGLAND; being a Fact-Book of English History. By F. A. WHITE, B.A. Seventh Edition, Corrected and Extended by H. A. DOBSON, Board of Trade. 2s. 6d. cloth.

'We do not remember to have seen anything of the kind so compendious, complete, accurate, and convenient for use.'—ATHENÆUM.

THE CIVIL SERVICE FIRST FRENCH BOOK: being a Practical First Course of French Grammar, with Exercises combined. By ACHILLE MOTTEAU. Fcp. 1s. 6d. cloth. (A KEY to the same, 2s. 6d.)

clear and compact little treatise.'—CIVILIAN. | 'Its arrangement is admirable.'—STANDARD.

THE CIVIL SERVICE ENGLISH GRAMMAR; being Notes on the History and Grammar of the English Language. By W. V. YATES, C.M. Second Edition, Revised, with Appendix containing Questions from Civil Service Examinations, with Model Answers. Fcp. 1s. 6d. cl.

'We cannot call to mind any single work which would render so much assistance to the student preparing to undergo examination.'—SCHOOL BOARD CHRONICLE.

THE CIVIL SERVICE BOOK-KEEPING; or, Book-keeping No Mystery: Its Principles Popularly Explained and the Theory of Double Entry Analysed. Fifth Edition. Fcp. 1s. 6d. cloth.

'It is clear and concise, and exactly such a text-book as students require.'—QUARTERLY JOURNAL OF EDUCATION.

THE CIVIL SERVICE CHRONOLOGY OF HISTORY, ART, LITERATURE, AND PROGRESS, from the Creation of the World to the Present Time. New Edition, with Continuation by W. D. HAMILTON, F.S.A., of H.M. Public Record Office. Fcp. 3s. 6d.

Accurate, wide, and thorough. Most useful to those who are reading up for examination.'—ENGLISH CHURCHMAN.

LOCKWOOD'S ELEMENTARY SCHOOL SERIES.

18mo, price 1s. each, strongly bound.

⁎ *The works in this cheap Elementary Series are designed to meet the requirements of Beginners, and are especially adapted to the capacities of the Young.*

THE ELEMENTS OF GEOGRAPHY. By the Rev B. G. JOHNS. New Edition, greaatly Enlarged and Revised throughout. 1s.

A SHORT AND SIMPLE HISTORY OF ENGLAND. By the Rev. B. G. JOHNS. New Edition, Enlarged and Corrected. 1s.

THE FRENCH LANGUAGE: An Easy and Practical Introduction to. By JOHN HAAS. (First Course.) Fifteenth Edition. 1s.

THE FRENCH LANGUAGE: An Easy and Practical Introduction to. By JOHN HAAS. (Second Course.) Tenth Edition. 1s. KEY to the Second Course. 1s. *⁎* *The First and Second Courses bound together*, 2s.

THE GERMAN LANGUAGE: The Little Scholar's First Step in. By Mrs. FALCK LEBAHN. 1s.

GERMAN READING: The Little Scholar's First Step in. By Mrs. FALCK LEBAHN. 1s.

THE GERMAN PREPOSITIONS, AND THE CASES THEY GOVERN: Exemplified in 2,500 Useful Colloquial Phrases. By S. GALINDO. 1s.

GERMAN COLLOQUIAL PHRASEOLOGY: Ememplifying all the Rules of the German Grammar, in more than 2,500 Phrases, with English Translations. By S. GALINDO. 1s.

OUTLINES OF THE HISTORY OF ROME. By the Rev. B. G. JOHNS. With Appendix. By the Rev. T. H. L. LEARY, D.C.L. 1s.

THE FIRST BOOK OF POETRY. By the Rev. B. G. JOHNS. 1s.

McHENRY'S SPANISH COURSE.

McHENRY'S SPANISH GRAMMAR. Containing the Elements of the Language and the Rules of Etymology and Syntax Exemplified; with Notes and Appendix, consisting of Dialogues, Select Poetry, Commercial Correspondence, Vocabulary, &c. New Edition. By A. ELWES. 12mo, 3s. 6d. cloth.

'The most complete Spanish Grammar for the use of Englishmen.' BRITISH HERALD.

McHENRY'S EXERCISES ON THE ETYMOLOGY, SYNTAX, IDIOMS, &c, of the Spanish Language. New Edition. By A. ELWES. 12mo, 3s. bound. *⁎* KEY to the EXERCISES, 4s.

'Unquestionably the best book of Spanish Exercises which has hitherto been published.'—GENTLEMAN'S MAGAZINE.

McHENRY'S SYNONYMS OF THE SPANISH LANGUAGE EXPLAINED. 12mo, 4s. bound.

'Anxious to render the work as interesting as possible; the Author has expended considerable time and labour in making a selection of characteristic extracts from the most approved writers, which, while they serve to exemplify or elucidate the particular synonyms under consideration, may at the same time recommend themselves to the learner by their intrinsic value.'—EXTRACT FROM THE PREFACE.

A NEW SPANISH GRAMMAR.

THE COMMERCIAL AND CONVERSATIONAL SPANISH GRAMMAR AND READER. A New and Practical Method of Learning the Spanish Language. By OSWALD KORTH, Professor of Languages, &c. Fcap. 8vo, 2s. 6d. cloth. [*Just published.*

'By means of the method Mr. Korth adopts, a student will be able in a very short time to obtain a thorough grasp of the Spanish language.'—CITY PRESS.

DR. LEBAHN'S POPULAR GERMAN SCHOOL BOOKS.

'*As an educational writer in the German tongue, Dr. Lebahn stands alone; none other has made even a distant approach to him.*'—BRITISH STANDARD.

LEBAHN'S GERMAN LANGUAGE IN ONE VOLUME.
Seventh Edition. Containing—I. A PRACTICAL GRAMMAR, with Exercises to every Rule. II. UNDINE: A Tale. By DE LA MOTTE FOUQUÉ. With Explanatory Notes of all Difficult Words and Phrases. III. A VOCABULARY OF 4,500 WORDS, synonymous in English and German. Crown 8vo. 8s. cloth. With Key, 10s. 6d. Key separate, 2s. 6d.

'The best German Grammar that has yet been published.'—MORNING POST.
'Had we to recommence the study of German, of all the German Grammars which we have examined—and they are not a few—we should unhesitatingly say, Falck Lebahn's is the book for us.'—EDUCATIONAL TIMES.

LEBAHN'S FIRST GERMAN COURSE.
New and Cheaper Edition (the Fifth). 12mo. 2s. cloth.

'It is hardly possible to have a simpler or better book for beginners in German.'—ATHENÆUM.

LEBAHN'S FIRST GERMAN READER.
New and Cheaper Edition (the Sixth). 12mo. 2s. cloth.

'An admirable book for beginners, which indeed may be used without a master.'—LEADER.

LEBAHN'S EXERCISES IN GERMAN.
Crown 8vo. 3s. 6d. cloth. Key to ditto, crown 8vo. 2s. 6d. cloth limp.

'A volume of "Exercises in German," including in itself all the vocabularies they require. The book is well planned; the selections for translation from German into English, or from English into German, being sometimes *curiously* well suited to the purpose for which they are taken.'—EXAMINER.

LEBAHN'S SELF-INSTRUCTOR IN GERMAN.
Crown 8vo. 3s. 6d. cloth.

'One of the most amusing elementary reading-books that ever passed under our hands.'
JOHN BULL

LEBAHN'S EDITION OF SCHMID'S HENRY VON EICHENFELS.
With Vocabulary and Familiar Dialogues. New and Cheaper Edition (the Eighth). Fcp. 8vo. 1s. 6d. cloth.

'The Dialogues are as perfectly adap'ed to render the student a speaker of this interesting language as is the Vocabulary for making him a reader.'—EDUCATIONAL TIMES.

LEBAHN'S GERMAN CLASSICS, with Notes and Complete Vocabularies.
Crown 8vo. 3s. 6d. each, cloth.

William Tell. A Drama, in Five Acts. By SCHILLER.

Goetz von Berlichingen. A Drama. By GOETHE.

Pagenstreiche: A Page's Frolics. A Comedy. By KOTZEBUE

Emilia Galotti. A Tragedy, in Five Acts. By LESSING.

Undine. A Tale. By FOUQUÉ.

Selections from the German Poets.

'With such aids, student will find no difficulty in these masterpieces.'
ATHENÆUM.

WORKS BY THE LATE JOSEPH PAYNE,
Of the College of Preceptors, &c.

PAYNE'S SELECT POETRY FOR CHILDREN, with brief Explanatory Notes, arranged for the use of Schools and Families. Twenty-second Edit. With fine Steel Frontispiece. 18mo, 2s. 6d. cl.
"We could wish for no better introduction to the study of poetry to place in the hands of our little ones."—*Schoolmaster.*

PAYNE'S STUDIES IN ENGLISH POETRY, with Biographical Sketches, and Notes Explanatory and Critical, a Text-Book for the Higher Classes of Schools. 9th Edition. Post 8vo, 3s. 6d.
"The selection is both extensive and varied, including many of the choicest specimens of English poetry."—*Eclectic Review.*

PAYNE'S STUDIES IN ENGLISH PROSE. Specimens of the Language in its various stages, with Notes Explanatory and Critical. Second Edition. Post 8vo, 3s. 6d. cloth.
"It is difficult to imagine a more useful manual."—*Scotsman.*

PAYNE'S STUDIES IN ENGLISH PROSE AND POETRY. Being the above two Books in 1 vol. 7s. 6d. half-bound.

FRENCH FOR VERY YOUNG BEGINNERS.

MOTTEAU'S ILLUSTRATED FRENCH AND ENGLISH TALK-BOOK; or, Petites Causeries: Being Elementary French and English Conversations. For Young Students and Home Teaching. With Models of Juvenile Correspondence. Fully Illustrated. By A. MOTTEAU. In Two Parts, 9d. each; or One Vol., 1s. 6d.
"For the admirable way in which it leads on young beginners, step by step, it would be impossible to surpass it."—*Civil Service Gazette.*

LA BAGATELLE; Intended to Introduce Children of Five or Six Years of Age to some Knowledge of the French Language. Revised by Madame N. L. Cheaper Edition. 18mo, 2s. bound.
"It is, indeed, French made very easy for very little children."—*The School.*

BARBAULD, LECONS POUR DES ENFANTS de l'Age de Deux Ans jusqu'à Cinq. Traduites de l'Anglais de Mme. BARBAULD par M. PASQUIER. Suivies des "Hymnes en Prose pour les Enfants." Nouvelle Edition, avec un Vocabulaire complet Français-Anglais. 18mo, 2s. cloth.

VOCABULAIRE SYMBOLIQUE ANGLO-FRANÇAIS—A SYMBOLIC FRENCH AND ENGLISH VOCABULARY, for Students of every age in all classes; in which the most Useful Words are taught by Illustrations. By L. C. RAGONOT. Twelfth Edition, with 850 Woodcuts and 9 full-page Copperplates. 4to, 3s. 6d. cloth.

CAMBRIDGE LOCAL EXAMINATIONS.

FRENCH EXAMINATION PAPERS set from 1881 to 1890, and the French Papers set for Commercial Certificates from 1888 to 1890. Edited, with Vocabularies and Explanatory Notes, by O. BAUMANN, B.A., Senior Modern Language Master at Wolverhampton Grammar School. Fcap. 8vo, 1s. 6d. cloth.

FRENCH SENTENCES AND SYNTAX. For Students entering the Oxford and Cambridge Local Examinations, College of Preceptors Examinations, Army Preliminary, &c. By O. BAUMANN, B.A. Fourth Edition, much Enlarged. Fcap. 8vo, 1s. cloth.

BOOKS ON THE ENGLISH LANGUAGE, etc.

ENGLAND, OUTLINES OF THE HISTORY OF; more especially with reference to the Origin and Progress of the English Constitution. A Text Book for Schools and Colleges. By WM. DOUGLAS HAMILTON, F.S.A., of H.M.'s Public Record Office. Fourth Edition, Revised. Maps and Woodcuts. 5s.; cloth boards, 6s.

THE SYNOPTICAL HISTORY OF ENGLAND. With the Contemporaneous Sovereigns and Events of General History, from the Earliest Records to the Year 1874. By L. C. BURT, Barrister-at-Law. Second and Cheaper Edition, oblong 4to, 5s. cloth.
"The book forms, probably, the most comprehensive and compact manual of English history ever published."—*Morning Post.*

GRAMMAR OF THE ENGLISH TONGUE, Spoken and Written. With an Introduction to the Study of Comparative Philology. By HYDE CLARKE, D.C.L. Fifth Edition. 1s. 6d.

DICTIONARY OF THE ENGLISH LANGUAGE, as Spoken and Written. Containing above 100,000 Words. By HYDE CLARKE, D.C.L. 3s. 6d.; cloth boards, 4s. 6d.; complete with the GRAMMAR, cloth boards, 5s. 6d.

THE YOUNG REPORTER. A Practical Guide to the Art and the Profession of Shorthand Writing, with a Dictionary of Latin Quotations, &c. Fcap., 1s. cloth.

EVENTS TO BE REMEMBERED IN THE HISTORY OF ENGLAND. A Series of Interesting Narratives of the most Remarkable Occurrences in each Reign. By CHARLES SELBY. Twenty-eighth Edition, Revised, with Additions. Crown 8vo, 350 pp. and 8 Plates, 2s. 6d. cloth.

TECHNICAL MEMORY: The Historical Lines of Dr. Grey's Technical Memory; with various Additions, chiefly as they apply to Modern History, arranged for General Use. Ninth Edition. 1s.

TRUTHS ILLUSTRATED BY GREAT AUTHORS: A Dictionary of nearly Four Thousand Aids to Reflection, Quotations of Maxims, Metaphors, Counsels, Cautions, Aphorisms, Proverbs, &c. &c. Compiled from Shakespeare and other Great Writers. Sixteenth Edition. Small crown 8vo, 564 pp., 3s. 6d. cloth.
"The quotations are perfect gems; their selection evinces sound judgment and an excellent taste."—*Dispatch.*
"We know of no better book of its kind."—*Examiner.*

COBWEBS TO CATCH FLIES; or, Dialogues in Short Sentences. Adapted for Children from the Age of Three to Eight Years. In Two Parts. Part I. Easy Lessons in Words of Three, Four, Five, and Six Letters, suited to Children from Three to Five Years of age. Part II. Short Stories for Children from Five to Eight Years of age. New Edition. Fcap. 8vo, 1s. cloth.

CHICKSEED WITHOUT CHICKWEED: Being very Easy and Entertaining Lessons for Little Children. Beautiful Frontispiece by ANELAY. 12mo, 1s. cloth.

NATURAL SCIENCE, etc.

THE VISIBLE UNIVERSE: Chapters on the Origin and Construction of the Heavens. By J. E. GORE, F.R.A.S., Author of "Star Groups," &c. Illustrated by 6 Stellar Photographs and 12 Plates. Demy 8vo, 16s. cloth.

"A valuable and lucid summary of recent astronomical theory, rendered more valuable and attractive by a series of stellar photographs and other illustrations."—*The Times.*

"In presenting a clear and concise account of the present state of our knowledge, Mr. Gore has made a valuable addition to the literature of the subject."—*Nature.*

"Mr. Gore's 'Visible Universe' is one of the finest works on astronomical science that has recently appeared in our language."—*Leeds Mercury.*

STAR GROUPS: A Student's Guide to the Constellations. By J. ELLARD GORE, F.R.A.S., M.R.I.A., &c., Author of "The Visible Universe," "The Scenery of the Heavens." With 30 Maps. Small 4to, 5s. cloth.

"A knowledge of the principal constellations visible in our latitudes may be easily acquired from the thirty maps and accompanying text contained in this work."—*Nature.*

"The volume contains thirty maps showing stars of the sixth magnitude—the usual naked eye limit—and each is accompanied by a brief commentary, adapted to facilitate recognition and bring to notice objects of special interest. For the purpose of a preliminary survey of the 'midnight pomp' of the heavens, nothing could be better than a set of delineations averaging scarcely twenty square inches in area, and including nothing that cannot at once be identified."—*Saturday Review.*

"A very compact and handy guide to the constellations."—*Athenæum.*

AN ASTRONOMICAL GLOSSARY; or, Dictionary of Terms used in Astronomy. With Tables of Data and Lists of Remarkable and Interesting Celestial Objects. By J. ELLARD GORE, F.R.A.S., Author of "The Visible Universe," &c. Small crown 8vo, 2s. 6d. cloth.

"A very useful little work for beginners in astronomy, and not to be despised by more advanced students."—*The Times.*

"A very handy book . . . the utility of which is much increased by its valuable tables of astronomical data."—*The Athenæum.*

"Astronomers of all kinds will be glad to have it for reference."—*Guardian.*

THE MICROSCOPE: Its Construction and Management. Including Technique, Photo-Micrography, and the Past and Future of the Microscope. By Dr. HENRI VAN HEURCK. Re-Edited and Augmented from the Fourth French Edition, and Translated by WYNNE E. BAXTER, F.G.S. 400 pages, with upwards of 250 Woodcuts, imp. 8vo, 18s. cloth.

"A translation of a well-known work, at once popular and comprehensive."—*Times.*

"The translation is as felicitous as it is accurate."—*Nature.*

PHOTO-MICROGRAPHY. By Dr. H. VAN HEURCK. Extracted from the above Work. Royal 8vo, with Illustrations, 1s. 6d.

THE TWIN RECORDS OF CREATION; or, Geology and Genesis, their Perfect Harmony and Wonderful Concord. By G. W. V. LE VAUX. 8vo, 5s. cloth.

"A valuable contribution to the evidences of Revelation, and disposes very conclusively of the arguments of those who would set God's Works against God's Word. No real difficulty is shirked, and no sophistry is left unexposed."—*The Rock.*

A SELECTION FROM THE LIST OF

Weale's Series,

EDUCATIONAL AND SCIENTIFIC.

☞ *These Popular and Cheap Series of Books, now comprising nearly Three Hundred and Fifty distinct works in almost every department of Science, Art and Education, are recommended to the notice of Literary and Scientific Institutions, Colleges, Schools, Science Classes, &c. &c.*

N.B. *Full lists will be forwarded on application.*

NATURAL PHILOSOPHY, etc.

PNEUMATICS, for the Use of Beginners. By CHARLES TOMLINSON. Fourth Edition, Enlarged. Illustrated. 1s. 6d.

MANUAL OF THE MOLLUSCA: A Treatise on Recent and Fossil Shells. By Dr. S. P. WOODWARD, A.L.S. Fourth Edition. With Appendix by RALPH TATE, A.L.S., F.G.S. With numerous Plates and 300 Woodcuts. 7s. 6d., cloth boards.

ASTRONOMY. By the late Rev. ROBERT MAYNE, M.A. Third Edition, by WILLIAM THYNNE LYNN, B.A., F.R.A.S. 2s.

STATICS AND DYNAMICS, the Principles and Practice of; embracing also a Clear Development of Hydrostatics, Hydrodynamics and Central Forces. By T. BAKER, C.E. 1s. 6d.

NATURAL PHILOSOPHY, Introduction to the Study of. By C. TOMLINSON. Woodcuts. 1s. 6d.

MECHANICS, Rudimentary Treatise on. By CHARLES TOMLINSON. Illustrated. 1s. 6d.

PHYSICAL GEOLOGY. Partly based on Major-General PORTLOCK'S "Rudiments of Geology." By RALPH TATE, A.L.S., &c. Woodcuts. 2s.

HISTORICAL GEOLOGY. Partly based on Major-General PORTLOCK'S "Rudiments." By RALPH TATE, A.L.S., &c. Woodcuts. 2s. 6d.

Natural Philosophy, etc.—*continued.*

RUDIMENTARY TREATISE ON GEOLOGY, Physical and Historical. Partly based on Major-General PORTLOCK'S "Rudiments of Geology." By RALPH TATE, A.L.S., F.G.S., &c. In One Volume. 4s. 6d.

ANIMAL PHYSICS, Handbook of. By Dr. LARDNER, D.C.L., formerly Professor of Natural Philosophy and Astronomy in University College, London. With 520 Illustrations. In One Vol. 7s. 6d. cloth boards.

ARITHMETIC, MATHEMATICS, etc.

MATHEMATICAL INSTRUMENTS. By J. F. HEATHER, M.A. Fourteenth Edition, Revised, with Additions by A. T. WALMISLEY, M.I.C.E. Original Edition, in One Vol. 2s.

** In ordering the above, be careful to say, 'Original Edition,' or give the number in the Series (32) to distinguish it from the Enlarged Edition in 3 vols.

LAND AND ENGINEERING SURVEYING. By T. BAKER, C.E. Revised by Professor J. R. YOUNG. Illustrated with Plates and Diagrams. 2s.; cloth boards, 2s. 6d.

READY RECKONER FOR THE ADMEASUREMENT OF LAND, including Tables showing the Price of Work from 2s. 6d. to £1 per Acre, and other useful Tables. By A. ARMAN, Fourth Edition, Corrected and Extended by C. NORRIS. 2s.

DESCRIPTIVE GEOMETRY: with a Theory of Shadows and of Perspective, extracted from the French of G. MONGE. By J. F. HEATHER, M.A. Illustrated with 14 Plates. 2s.

PRACTICAL PLANE GEOMETRY. By J. F. HEATHER, M.A. With 215 Woodcuts. 2s.

COMMERCIAL BOOK-KEEPING. With Commercial Phrases and Forms in English, French, Italian, and German. By JAMES HADDON, M.A. London. 1s. 6d.

ARITHMETIC. By Professor J. R. YOUNG. Tenth Edition. Corrected. 1s. 6d.

    A KEY to the above, containing Solutions in full to the Exercises, together with Comments, Explanations, and Improved Processes, for the Use of Teachers and Unassisted Learners. By J. R. YOUNG. 1s. 6d.

EQUATIONAL ARITHMETIC, applied to Questions of Interest, Annuities, Life Assurance, and General Commerce; with various Tables. By W. HIPSLEY. 2s.

ALGEBRA, THE ELEMENTS OF. By JAMES HADDON, M.A. 2s.

    A KEY AND COMPANION to the above Book, forming an extensive repository of Solved Examples and Problems in Illustration of the various Expedients necessary in Algebraical Operations. Especially adapted for Self-Instruction. By J. R. YOUNG. 1s. 6d.

Arithmetic, Mathematics, etc.—*continued.*

EUCLID: with many Additional Propositions and Explanatory Notes; to which is prefixed an Introductory Essay on Logic. By HENRY LAW, C.E. 2s. 6d.; cloth boards, 3s.

₊ *Sold also separately, viz:*
EUCLID. The First Three Books. By HENRY LAW, C.E. 1s. 6d.
EUCLID. Books iv., v., vi., xi., xii. By HENRY LAW, C.E. 1s. 6d.

ANALYTICAL GEOMETRY AND CONIC SECTIONS. By JAMES HANN. Revised by Professor J. R. YOUNG. 2s.; cloth boards, 2s. 6d.

PLANE TRIGONOMETRY. By JAMES HANN. 1s. 6d.

SPHERICAL TRIGONOMETRY. By JAMES HANN. Revised by CHARLES H. DOWLING, C.E. 1s.

₊ *Or with "The Elements of Plane Trigonometry," in One Vol., 2s. 6d.*

MENSURATION AND MEASURING. By T. BAKER, C.E. Revised by E. NUGENT, C.E. Illustrated. 1s. 6d.

INTEGRAL CALCULUS. By HOMERSHAM COX, B.A. 1s.

DIFFERENTIAL CALCULUS, Elements of the. By W. S. B. WOOLHOUSE, F.R.A.S., &c. 1s. 6d.

ARITHMETIC. By JAMES HADDON, M.A. Revised by ABRAHAM ARMAN. 1s. 6d.

A KEY TO HADDON'S ARITHMETIC. By A. ARMAN. 1s. 6d.

THE SLIDE RULE, and How to Use It. By C. HOARE, C.E. With a Slide Rule in tuck of cover. 2s. 6d.; cloth boards, 3s.

DRAWING AND MEASURING INSTRUMENTS. By J. F. HEATHER, M.A. Illustrated. 1s. 6d.

OPTICAL INSTRUMENTS. By J. F. HEATHER. 1s. 6d.

SURVEYING AND ASTRONOMICAL INSTRUMENTS. By J. F. HEATHER, M.A. Illustrated. 1s. 6d.

₊ *The above Three Volumes form an Enlargement of the Author's original work, "Mathematical Instruments: their Construction, Adjustment, Testing, and Use," the Fourteenth Edition of which is on sale, price 2s. (See No. 32 in the Series.)*

MATHEMATICAL INSTRUMENTS. By J. F. HEATHER. Enlarged Edition, for the most part entirely Re-written. The Three Parts as above in One thick Volume. With numerous Illustrations, 4s. 6d.; cloth boards, 5s.

THE COMPLETE MEASURER. Compiled for Timber-growers, Merchants, and Surveyors, Stonemasons, Architects, and others. By RICHARD HORTON. Fifth Edition. 4s.; leather, 5s.

THEORY OF COMPOUND INTEREST AND ANNUITIES. With Tables of Logarithms. By FEDOR THOMAN, of the Société Crédit Mobilier, Paris. 4s.

Arithmetic, Mathematics, etc.—*continued*.

THE COMPENDIOUS CALCULATOR ; or, Easy and Concise Methods of Performing the various Arithmetical Operations required in Commercial and Business Transactions. By DANIEL O'GORMAN. Corrected and Extended by Professor J. R. YOUNG. Twenty-seventh Edition. Carefully Revised by C. NORRIS. 2s. 6d. ; cloth boards, 3s. 6d.

MATHEMATICAL TABLES, for Trigonometrical, Astronomical, and Nautical Calculations ; to which is prefixed a Treatise on Logarithms. By HENRY LAW, C.E. Together with a Series of Tables for Navigation and Nautical Astronomy. By Professor J. R. YOUNG. New Edition. 4s. ; cloth boards, 4s. 6d.

LOGARITHMS. With Mathematical Tables for Trigonometrical, Astronomical, and Nautical Calculations. By H. LAW, C.E. Revised Edition (forming part of the above work). 3s.

MEASURES, WEIGHTS AND MONEYS OF ALL NATIONS, and an Analysis of the Christian, Hebrew, and Mahometan Calendars. By W. S. B. WOOLHOUSE, F.R.A.S., F.S.S., &c. Seventh Edition, Revised and Enlarged. 2s. 6d.; cloth boards, 3s.

MATHEMATICS AS APPLIED TO THE CONSTRUCTIVE ARTS. Illustrating the various processes of Mathematical Investigation, by means of Arithmetical and Simple Algebraical Equations and Practical Examples ; also the Methods of Analysing Principles and Deducing Rules and Formulæ, applicable to the Requirements of Practice. By FRANCIS CAMPIN, C.E. 3s. ; cloth boards, 3s. 6d.

ENGLISH LANGUAGE, etc.

GRAMMAR OF THE ENGLISH TONGUE. By HYDE CLARKE, D.C.L. Fourth Edition. 1s. 6d.

DICTIONARY OF THE ENGLISH LANGUAGE. Containing above 130,000 Words. By HYDE CLARKE, D.C.L. 3s. 6d. ; cloth boards, 4s. 6d. ; complete with the GRAMMAR, cloth bds. 5s. 6d.

COMPOSITION AND PUNCTUATION. By JUSTIN BRENAN. Eighteenth Edition. 1s. 6d.

DERIVATIVE SPELLING-BOOK. By J. ROWBOTHAM. F.R.A.S. Improved Edition. 1s. 6d.

THE ART OF EXTEMPORE SPEAKING : Hints for the Pulpit, the Senate, and the Bar. By M. BAUTAIN. Translated from the French. Eighth Edition. 2s. 6d.

PLACES AND FACTS IN POLITICAL AND PHYSICAL GEOGRAPHY. By the Rev. EDGAR RAND, B.A. 1s.

LOGIC, *Pure and Applied.* By S. H. EMMENS. 1s. 6d.

HISTORY.

ENGLAND, OUTLINES OF THE HISTORY OF; more especially with reference to the Origin and Progress of the English Constitution. By WILLIAM DOUGLAS HAMILTON, F.S.A. Fourth Edition. Maps and Woodcuts. 5s.; cloth boards, 6s.

GREECE, OUTLINES OF THE HISTORY OF. By W. DOUGLAS HAMILTON, F.S.A., and EDWARD LEVIEN, M.A. 2s. 6d.; cloth boards, 3s. 6d.

ROME, OUTLINES OF THE HISTORY OF. By EDWARD LEVIEN, M.A. Map, 2s. 6d.; cloth boards, 3s. 6d.

CHRONOLOGY OF HISTORY, ART, LITERATURE, AND PROGRESS, from the Creation of the World to the Present Time. New Edition, with Continuation by W. D. HAMILTON, F.S.A. 3s. cloth boards, 3s. 6d.

LATIN.

LATIN GRAMMAR. By the Rev. THOMAS GOODWIN, M.A. 1s. 6d.

LATIN-ENGLISH DICTIONARY. By the Rev. THOMAS GOODWIN, M.A. 2s.

ENGLISH-LATIN DICTIONARY. By the Rev. THOMAS GOODWIN, M.A. 1s. 6d.

LATIN DICTIONARY (as above). Complete in One Vol., 3s. 6d.; cloth boards, 4s. 6d.

_{*} Or with the Grammar, cloth beards, 5s. 6d.

LATIN CLASSICS.

With Explanatory Notes in English.

LATIN DELECTUS. By H. YOUNG. 1s. 6d.

CÆSARIS COMMENTARII DE BELLO GALLICO. With Notes and Geographical Register. By H. YOUNG. 2s.

CICERONIS ORATIO PRO SEXTO ROSCIO AMERINO. By the Rev. JAMES DAVIES, M.A. 1s. 6d.

CICERONIS ORATIONES IN CATILINAM, VERREM, ET PRO ARCHIA. By Rev. T. H. L. LEARY, D.C.L., Oxford. 1s. 6d.

CICERONIS CATO MAJOR, LÆLIUS, BRUTUS SIVE DE SENECTUTE, DE AMICITIA, DE CLARIS ORATORIBUS DIALOGI. By W. SMITH, M.A., F.R.G.S. 2s.

CORNELIUS NEPOS. By H. YOUNG. 1s.

HORACE: ODES, EPODES, AND CARMEN SÆCULARE By H. YOUNG. 1s. 6d.

HORACE: SATIRES, EPISTLES, and ARS POETICA. By W. BROWNRIGG SMITH, M.A., F.R.G.S. 1s. 6d.

Latin Classics—*continued.*

JUVENALIS SATIRÆ. By T. H. S. Escott, B.A. 2s.

LIVY: HISTORY OF ROME. By H. Young and W. B. Smith, M.A. Part 1. Books i., ii., 1s. 6d.
——————— Part 2. Books iii., iv., v., 1s. 6d.
——————— Part 3. Books xxi., xxii., 1s. 6d.

SALLUSTII CRISPI CATALINA ET BELLUM JUGURTHINUM. By W. M. Donne, B.A. Trin. Coll. Cam. 1s. 6d.

TERENTII ADELPHI, HECYRA, PHORMIO. Edited by the Rev. James Davies, M.A. 2s.

TERENTII ANDRIA ET HEAUTONTIMORUMENOS. By the Rev. James Davies, M.A. 1s. 6d.

TERENTII EUNUCHUS, COMŒDIA. By the Rev. J. Davies, M.A. 1s. 6d.

VIRGILII MARONIS BUCOLICA ET GEORGICA. The Bucolics by W. Rushton, M.A., and the Georgics by H. Young. 1s. 6d.

VIRGILII MARONIS ÆNEIS. By H. Young and Rev. T. H. L. Leary, D.C.L. 3s.
——————— Part 1. Books i.–vi., 1s. 6d.
——————— Part 2. Books vii.–xii., 2s.

LATIN VERSE SELECTIONS from Catullus, Tibullus, Propertius, and Ovid. By W. B. Donne, M.A. 2s.

LATIN PROSE SELECTIONS from Varro, Columella, Vitruvius, Seneca, Quintilian, Florus, Velleius, Paterculus, Valerius Maximus, Suetonius, Apuleius, &c. By W. B. Donne, M.A. 2s.

GREEK.

GREEK GRAMMAR. By Hans Claude Hamilton. 1s. 6d.

GREEK LEXICON. By Henry R. Hamilton. Vol. 1. Greek-English, 2s. 6d.; Vol. 2. English-Greek, 2s. Or the Two Vols. in One, 4s. 6d.; cloth boards, 5s.

GREEK LEXICON (as above). Complete, with the Grammar, in One Vol., cloth boards, 6s.

GREEK CLASSICS.

With Explanatory Notes in English.

GREEK DELECTUS. By H. Young and John Hutchinson, M.A., of the High School, Glasgow. 1s. 6d.

ÆSCHYLUS. PROMETHEUS VINCTUS. By the Rev. James Davies, M.A. 1s.

ÆSCHYLUS. SEPTEM CONTRA THEBES. By the Rev. James Davies, M.A. 1s.

ARISTOPHANES. ACHARNIANS. By C. S. T. Townshend, M.A. 1s. 6d.

Greek Classics—*continued*.

EURIPIDES: ALCESTIS. By JOHN MILNER, B.A. 1s. 6d.

EURIPIDES: HECUBA AND MEDEA. By W. BROWN-RIGG SMITH, M.A., F.R.G.S. 1s. 6d.

HERODOTUS, THE HISTORY OF, chiefly after the Text of GAISFORD. By T. H. L. LEARY, M.A., D.C.L.
Part 1. Books i., ii. (The CLIO and EUTERPE), 2s.
Part 2. Books iii., iv. (The THALIA and MELPOMENE), 2s.
Part 3. Books v.-vii. (The TERPSICHORE, ERATO, and POLYHYMNIA), 2s.
Part 4. Books viii., ix. (The URANIA and CALLIOPE) and Index, 1s. 6d.

HOMER, THE WORKS OF. By T. H. L. LEARY, M.A., D.C.L.

THE ILIAD.
Part 1. Books i. to vi., 1s. 6d.
Par 2. Books vii. to xii., 1s. 6d.
Part 3. Books xiii. to xviii., 1s. 6d.
Part 4. Books xix. to xxiv., 1s. 6d.

THE ODYSSEY.
Part 1. Books i. to vi., 1s. 6d.
Part 2. Books vii. to xii., 1s. 6d.
Part 3. Books xiii. to xviii., 1s. 6d.
Part 4. Books xix. to xxiv. and Hymns, 2s.

LUCIAN'S SELECT DIALOGUES. By H. YOUNG. 1s. 6d.

PLATO'S DIALOGUES: The Apology of Socrates, the Crito, and the Phædo. By the Rev. JAMES DAVIES, M.A. 2s.

SOPHOCLES. ŒDIPUS TYRANNUS. By H. YOUNG. 1s.

SOPHOCLES. ANTIGONE. By the Rev. JOHN MILNER, B.A. 2s.

THUCYDIDES. HISTORY OF THE PELOPONNESIAN WAR. By H. YOUNG. Book 1. 1s. 6d.

XENOPHON'S ANABASIS. By H. YOUNG. Part 1. Books i. to iii., 1s. Part 2. Books iv. to vii., 1s.

XENOPHON'S AGESILAUS. By LL. F. W. JEWITT. 1s. 6d.

DEMOSTHENES: The Oration on the Crown and the Philippics. By Rev. T. H. L. LEARY. 1s. 6d.

FRENCH.

FRENCH GRAMMAR. By G. L. STRAUSS, Ph.D. 1s. 6d.

FRENCH-ENGLISH DICTIONARY. By ALFRED ELWES. 1s. 6d.

ENGLISH-FRENCH DICTIONARY. By ALFRED ELWES. 2s.

FRENCH DICTIONARY (as above). Complete in One Vol., 3s.; cloth boards, 3s. 6d.
** Or with the GRAMMAR, cloth boards, 4s. 6d.

FRENCH AND ENGLISH PHRASE BOOK. Containing Introductory Lessons, with Translations, for the convenience of Students, several Vocabularies of Words, a Collection of suitable Phrases and Easy Familiar Dialogues. 1s. 6d.

GERMAN.

GERMAN GRAMMAR. By Dr. G. L. STRAUSS. 1s. 6d.

GERMAN READER: A Series of Extracts, carefully culled from the most approved Authors of Germany. By G. L. STRAUSS, Ph.D. 1s.

GERMAN TRIGLOT DICTIONARY. By NICHOLAS ESTERHAZY S. A. HAMILTON. In Three Parts. Part 1, German French-English. Part 2, English-German-French. Part 3, French-German-English. 3s., or cloth boards, 4s.

GERMAN TRIGLOT DICTIONARY (as above), together with German Grammar (No. 39), in One Volume, cloth boards, 5s.

ITALIAN.

ITALIAN GRAMMAR. By ALFRED ELWES. 1s. 6d.

ITALIAN TRIGLOT DICTIONARY. By ALFRED ELWES. Vol. 1. Italian-English-French. 2s. 6d.

ITALIAN TRIGLOT DICTIONARY. By ALFRED ELWES. Vol. 2. English-French-Italian. 2s. 6d.

ITALIAN TRIGLOT DICTIONARY. By ALFRED ELWES. Vol. 3. French-Italian-English. 2s. 6d.

ITALIAN TRIGLOT DICTIONARY (as above). In One Vol., cloth boards, 7s. 6d.

** Or with the ITALIAN GRAMMAR, cloth boards, 8s. 6d.

SPANISH AND PORTUGUESE.

SPANISH GRAMMAR. By ALFRED ELWES. 1s. 6d.

SPANISH-ENGLISH AND ENGLISH-SPANISH DICTIONARY. By ALFRED ELWES. 4s.; cloth boards, 5s.

** Or with the GRAMMAR, cloth boards, 6s.

PORTUGUESE GRAMMAR. By ALFRED ELWES, Author of "A Spanish Grammar," &c. 1s. 6d.

PORTUGUESE - ENGLISH AND ENGLISH - PORTUGUESE DICTIONARY. By ALFRED ELWES. Second Edition, Revised. 5s.; cloth boards, 6s.

** Or with the GRAMMAR, cloth boards, 7s.

HEBREW.

HEBREW GRAMMAR. By Dr. BRESSLAU. 1s. 6d.

HEBREW AND ENGLISH DICTIONARY, BIBLICAL AND RABBINICAL. By Dr. BRESSLAU. 6s.

ENGLISH AND HEBREW DICTIONARY. By Dr. BRESSLAU. 3s.

HEBREW DICTIONARY (as above), in Two Vols. Complete with the GRAMMAR, cloth boards, 12s.

OGDEN, SMALE AND CO. LIMITED, PRINTERS, GREAT SAFFRON HILL,

www.ingramcontent.com/pod-product-compliance
Lightning Source LLC
Chambersburg PA
CBHW020817230426
43666CB00007B/1045